KHRUSHCHEV'S SHOE

Roy Underhill

Khrushchev's Shoe

and Other Ways to Captivate
Audiences from One to One Thousand

Perseus Publishing
Cambridge, Massachusetts

CL
808.51
c.1
10/13

Library of Congress Catalogue information is available.
Includes bibliographical references and index.
ISBN 0-7382-0672-5

Perseus Publishing is a member of the Perseus Books Group

Perseus Publishing books are available at special discounts for bulk purchases in the U.S. by corporations, institutions, and other organizations. For more information, please contact the Special Markets Department at the Perseus Books Group, 11 Cambridge Center, Cambridge, MA 02142, or call (617) 252-5298.

Find us on the World Wide Web at
http://www.perseuspublishing.com

1 2 3 4 5 6 7 8 9 10   04 03 02
First paperback printing, May 2002

To the memory of Mattie Rachel Underhill
who taught us all the important things.

CONTENTS

Acknowledgments

There is a joke that the French allegedly tell on themselves. Seeing something succeed, their response is "Well, yes, it works in practice. But—will it work in theory?" That's the position I've been in as I have sought to square my experience relative to the scientific literature on the psychology of communication. I acknowledge the scholars in the notes and bibliography, but my first thanks go to the thousands of audiences who patiently showed me what they need.

I have also learned from many presenters, and particularly from those who graciously allowed me to interview them on their craft. Thanks to Bill Barker, Gary Brumfield, Rex Ellis, Jeremy Fried, Mack Headley, Christy Coleman Matthews, Noel Poirier, Tim Russell, Kristen Spivey, Robert Watson Jr., Garland Wood, Marcus Hansen and George Hassel.

Many presentation professionals also generously discussed this project with me. Thanks to Margie Weiler, Sarah Caramia, Peter Ross, Stacy Roth, Pam Pettengell, and Judy Kristoffersen whose insights into the nature of audiences are found throughout this book.

Much of the material in this book found its earliest form as handouts for workshop participants. I am indebted to the sponsors of these classes for their support and guidance, as well as for trusting me with their students. Thanks to Ralph Ward; Karen Gale of Georgetown University; Keni Sturgeon of the Chesapeake Bay Maritime Museum; Lynn Dierking, John Falk, Jessica Luke, and Dale Jones of the Institute for Learning Innovation; Edward Baker and Susan Funk of Mystic Seaport Museum; Claire Mehalick at the Richmond Children's Museum; Jim Parker of the Alabama Historical Commission; Connie Weinzapfel of Historic New Harmony; Joan Hoge of the Historical Society of Talbot County; and John Caramia, Conny Graft, Christy Coleman Matthews, and Robyn Scouse of the Colonial Williamsburg Foundation. Some of the early research for this book was supported by Earl Soles and Dennis O'Toole.

For any book to survive its journey requires thoughtful guardians. I thank my representative Andrea Pedolsky and editor Jacqueline Murphy for their creative energy in bringing this one safely home.

Books become obsessions which can make you very dull company. My family, Jane, Rachell, and Eleanor, took the brunt of the grind and were ever helpful in every way.

Friends generously agreed to read early stages of this book and lend their advice and encouragement. Thanks to Nan Rothwell, Linda Maloof, David Perry, Ron Wheeler, Pam Pettengell, and Ann Browning. Later versions of the book benefited greatly from the council of Stacy Roth, Sister Barbara Ann Underhill, Judy Kristoffersen, and Christopher Wilson of the Henry Ford Museum & Greenfield Village. Of course, the errors are my own.

KHRUSHCHEV'S SHOE

A story, in which native humour reigns,
Is often useful, always entertains;
A graver fact, enlisted on your side,
May furnish illustration, well applied;
But sedentary weavers of long tales
Give me the fidgets, and my patience fails.
A tale should be judicious, clear, succinct;
The language plain, and incidents well link'd;
Tell not as new what ev'ry body knows;
And, new or old, still hasten to a close.

William Cowper, *Conversation*, 1782

CHAPTER 1
MINDS ON!

Success with an audience is one of life's great pleasures. During my years as a craftsman in a historic village, I grew to deeply enjoy interacting with audiences. Of course I was fearful when I was new to the task—everyone is—but the folks I encountered every day were intelligent and interested. They had traveled long distances and paid good money to have a pleasurably enlightening experience. They had made an investment in having a good time, and I learned that they would teach you how to succeed—if you paid attention—if you took a few chances. You could discover the rules of engagement.

One of the features that people enjoyed most were "hands-on" experiences. Letting them touch things and do things engaged their senses and caused faces to light up in ways you never saw when they were just passive recipients of your presentation. But there were other times you saw that same expression, when the mental gears were turning in synchrony with yours, times when their intelligence was engaged, when they entered a "minds-on" state of pleasurable cognition. Their hands may have been empty, but their brains were fingering treasures with delight. Bingo! That was the target.

I knew what I was shooting for, but I also came to learn that it was a constantly moving target. To engage the intelligence of your audience, you must constantly engage your own, and it can be hard work, and frustrating. One way to survive this school of experience is to find a positive twist to every turn. In fact, it was a negative reaction that led me to a most positive perspective. One of my apprentices, impatient with the questions of an endless stream of "touristas," summed up his feelings about their intelligence with this pronouncement: "Body on vacation—mind on vacation." I laughed, but the phrase stuck in my mind. Perhaps that is how we *should* think of our audience. A body on vacation likes to do new things: A mind on vacation likes to do new *thinks*.

When people go on vacation, they free themselves to do things that are outside of their workaday experience. They swim, they fish, they hike, they ski down a mountain. It's new, it's different, it's challenging. So too, when they take their minds on vacation, they want rewarding, new experiences. These new adventures can be even more satisfying when they have someone to guide them along. That's where you come in. Whether you are an executive giving potential investors a factory tour, a trainer showing employees how to use a new software product, or you are just conversing with friends over dinner, you can engage the intelligence of your audience, rewarding their brains just as if they had traveled to a fascinating and unforgettable place. There are rewards in this for you as well. Nothing can be so pleasurably terrifying as to be the leader of intelligence—to succeed with an audience. It's success that the audience shares with you, success that comes with study and practice, success that you deserve for taking your work with your audience seriously.

Intelligences all around us, as well as our own, search desperately for such engagement. We humans, for survival's sake, always strive to reduce our uncertainty about the world around us. Work and play are both means of reducing that uncertainty. Work puts food on the table, but play gives us a survival advantage through exercise and experience. We manipulate objects, turn over rocks, look in medicine cabinets to find out more about our environment. This may lead us to a new source of food, a new way of attaching a rock to a stick, or to better understand and hence to better compete or cooperate with our neighbors. When we play, we manipulate our environment to discover new connections and behaviors that may, or may not, be useful in our work. We can learn from our mistakes without paying a "real-world" penalty. The end is not to put food on the table, to defend the cave, to raise the baby—but to become better at doing so. Evolution has attached pleasurable sensations to this playful use of our body and brain, just as it has with other activities that more obviously ensure the perpetuation of the species. This state of playful, pleasurable learning is the *minds on* state.

Minds on is a playful state of mind but a serious business. Unlike painting and sculpture where you labor alone and then place your work before an audience that can take it or leave it, lame presentations can steal millions of hours from the lives of others, igniting or extinguishing a lifetime of interest. Success with an audience cannot only change lives, it can even save them. What could be more serious than vital safety instructions? Yet even the Federal Aviation Administration recognizes that more humorous and inventive "seatbelt and exit" instructions from the flight attendant do the job better than the same old recitation.

It's serious, but it doesn't need to be grim. Your audience must enjoy their voyage as you guide them between the twin hazards of boredom and dazzling distraction. The rewards must be part of the journey, not something they get only when they arrive. When the experience is really working, they are not just sleeping passengers, they are active members of the crew. Your hand may be on the tiller, but your audience has work to do too, a kind of work that is as rewarding and pleasurable as play.

For your audience, the pleasure is in their own achievement, in taking that next step beyond. In his 1739 "Treatise on Human Nature" philosopher David Hume wrote that even the knowledge of truth is not as pleasurable as "the genius and capacity which is employed in its invention and discovery. What is easy and obvious is never valued; and even what is *in itself* difficult, if we come to the knowledge of it without difficulty, and without any stretch of thought or judgment, it is but little regarded." In other words, we don't spend a lot of money on pre-assembled jigsaw puzzles. Archimedes ran naked through the streets of Syracuse shouting "Eureka!" not because he saw the answer to a vexing problem written on someone else's wax tablet; he was excited because through *his* personal struggle *he* found it.

The greatest pleasure, that zone of growth for your audience, lies just beyond that which has already been achieved, where they are not bored by tasks that are too easy, but neither are they overly stressed by challenges that are too hard. Like coaching a weightlifter, you add just enough cerebral challenge to build their strength, but not enough to hurt or discourage them. Reaching this state of optimal experience together requires a dynamic balance of challenging goals with responsiveness to feedback.

Your role in bringing people to this golden zone is best illustrated in the graphic matrix on the facing page devised by Laurent Daloz in his *Effective Teaching and Mentoring*. A combination of high support and high challenge promotes growth through successfully engaged intelligence. In offering growth, your ultimate success is measured by the extent to which you create a desire for continued

Retreat · High · Growth

Low —— Support —— High

Challenge

Low

Stasis · Confirmation

Laurent Daloz's matrix of challenge and support illustrates the role of the mentor in fostering growth.

growth. This is harder than we might think. Growth means giving up some old ideas. It's a little death, and the surviving beliefs need to go through the steps of grieving. As inventor Edwin Land once said, "New ideas are easy, getting rid of the old ones is hard."

But that's what your audience likes—playful challenging work for the body and brain. Now how do you bottle and sell it? How do you create an environment that provokes and rewards curiosity at every turn? First, you must provide a wealth and variety of interesting opportunities for the audience to play with new ideas that lie just beyond what is already comfortable for them. Second, you give your audience enough tools and material to work with so that they can reasonably succeed if they try.

Your work is to read the stress level of the audience to see when it is too hard or too easy and adjust it accordingly. You must let them earn the rewards for their adventurous spirit and their trust in you. They need to reduce their uncertainty, not only about the outside world, but also about themselves. This takes sensitivity, watching, adjusting, practicing, and persevering as you get better and better at it. You learn to adjust the balance of challenge and support so they can do their work of growing as individuals. Get it right and they will get the most out of the experience, and so will you.

This is not to say that you should eliminate all uncertainty, that you should guarantee the success of the audience at every turn. You have plenty of your own work to do, so don't steal theirs. It is the very failure of the audience to immediately comprehend that drives them to learn. Difficult and complex subjects must retain some of their obdurate nature to keep their meaning. Landing on the top of Mount Everest in a helicopter is not the same as climbing it. Sometimes to fail in the attempt is to succeed in understanding. Be sure, however, that any difficulty is truly integral to the objective, not imposed on it by the presenter's bias, ignorance, laziness, or self-indulgence. Get your audience's intelligence working on *good* problems related to the subject, not on trying to sort out useless problems created by a confusing presentation.

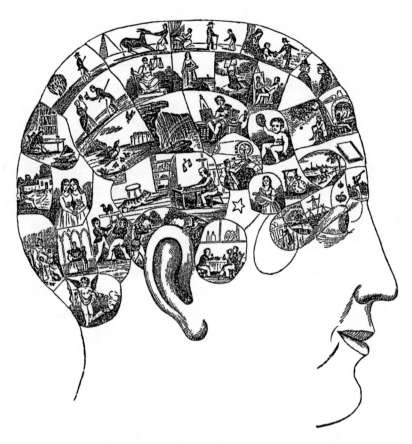

We are an intelligent species and the use of our intelligence
quite properly gives us pleasure. In this respect the brain is like a muscle. When
we think well, we feel good. Understanding is a kind of ecstasy.

Carl Sagan

The Pleasures of Intelligence

So what is this intelligence stuff anyway? Psychologist Steven Pinker defines it as "the ability to obtain goals in the face of obstacles by means of decisions based on rational (truth-obeying) rules." Powerful communication puts intelligence to work overcoming obstacles to obtain goals. But where are the handles of this intelligence machine? A theory that slices intelligence into eight parts proposed by psychologist Robert J. Sternberg is the most useful to us. Allowing your audience to successfully engage, rather than frustrate, these areas of intelligence is the best way of allowing them to enjoy themselves. Here's how you might lead an engaging experience exercising each of these intelligences, thus giving your audience a little burst of pleasure in their undertaking.

Help Them Use Their Internal Intelligence

Planning: Give your audience orientation resources, by telling them how long your program is going to last, when you will take a break and any location information so they can allocate their time and energy intelligently.

Cognitive Tasks: Provide a variety of opportunities for the audience to use their traditional thinking skills in making comparisons, generalizations, getting jokes, seeing connections, making predictions.

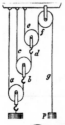

Discovery: Allow for the acquisition of new knowledge by providing a wide variety of new words and images. Embed these new ideas within familiar ideas to aid understanding. Present mysteries as well as contextual clues to their solution.

Help Them Use Their Experience Intelligence

Novelty: Put people into new sets of rules and objectives. Whether it be a business simulation or a historical role-play, the exercise of new concepts and ways of thinking challenges their ability to deal with novelty. Let them try new things.

Automating Skills: Give the folks time to integrate the information and get reasonably good at it. Don't constantly change the rules so that skills learned earlier no longer apply.

Help Them Use Their Environmental Intelligence

Adapting: Present an environment where the requirements for optimal engagement are clear, reasonable, and minimal. Be sure that they can reasonably adapt themselves to it.

Shaping: Allow for reshaping by responding to the expressed needs of the audience. Tune into the feedback channels and make deliberate choices. Offer time for questions and special requests, allowing them the freedom to explore their own interests and level of challenge.

Choosing: Inform your potential audience about the nature of your program beforehand so that they are with you by choice and not by mistake. Offer significant variety when "fishing" for areas of interest. Should they want to go elsewhere, give them a way to do so.

Again, the quality of the experience you present depends on the degree to which you reward or frustrate these intelligences. Consider an example from the domain of knowledge acquisition through discovery. On a tour of a small museum, you are shown a kitchen fireplace with a display of antique hearth-cooking devices. One of the devices is a cast iron, grapefruit-sized sphere mounted on a shaft with a crank on one end. What is this thing? Your guide chooses to make this a guessing game where she withholds the correct information until you are defeated. You have to keep guessing until you are ready to "Give up." Only then will she triumphantly tell you that the mysterious object is a coffee roaster.

How different the experience would have been if she had chosen to give you the tools and then let you work. What if she had said, "Have you ever seen one of these before?" "What is it? Well, open it up and see what's inside." Opening the device, you find it is half filled with green coffee beans. Now you have all the clues to answer your own question—fire, green coffee beans, and an iron container that rotates before the fire. "Oh! It's a coffee roaster!" You are pleased with your discovery rather than humiliated by your failure. Your brain releases endorphins and dopamine. You want to come back to this source of pleasure rather than avoid this source of pain. It's as simple as that.

Exploring new ideas and environments is the work of your audience. You must make this work more rewarding by generously and constantly enriching the environment—whether it be a conversation or an industrial exhibit—with strange words or intriguing objects that spark the interchange. These interesting intellectual and physical highlights can also serve as a menu of openings for your audience to choose among. Many presenters who work interactively call these tools "hooks," tempting curiosities to spark interest. If they nibble at the hook, you can explore it further. If they don't, you just keep moving.

Although the encounters I am focusing on are relatively short, perhaps measured in minutes, not days or months, the honored role of the mentor still applies. As Laurent Daloz says of Dante's guide through the underworld, the mentor's role is "engendering trust, issuing a challenge, providing encouragement, and offering a vision for the journey." What's true of Hades can also be true of a winery tour or a summation to the jury—the experience gains clarity and direction with an intelligent guide. These presentations are usually encounters with strangers, so part of the work is building trust toward the transformational moment when they accept you as their guide. As your skills grow you will constantly be encountering yourself as a stranger as well. You continuously will face transformational moments of accepting yourself as a trustworthy guide on your own journey of professional growth.

As we begin our own exploration through these pages, let me better define the territory I intend to travel through. The words *guide,*

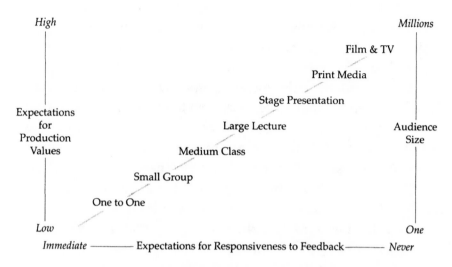

*Audiences have reasonable expectations for responsiveness and "polish"
based on the medium and the scale of the event.*

mentor, professional, and *audience* that I have been using—all imply an unequal relationship between you and the others in the shared communication. This is bigger than conversation, and smaller than the big presentation. It is about presentations that seem like conversations because they are informal and interactive, and about conversations that stand out as especially rewarding. I am concentrating on the middle area of the chart above, where interactive presentation combines the best of both ends of the scale. It is well informed, nimble in response, and elegantly experienced in delivery. As Francis Bacon observed, reading makes you full, conversation makes you ready, and writing makes you exact. It is just this combination of fullness, readiness, and exactness that makes you a worthy leader.

As for the followers, for lack of a better word, I will call them the audience throughout this work. A better word might not emphasize "audio"—listening to words—as much, but that is the channel we tend to use. Humans most efficiently engage with the world by watching real things and listening to verbal commentary—I show you how to make the spear point as I tell you why I chose this particular stone. You ask questions, I respond. I let you try it and coach you with words. Later, when we are apart, the combination of words, visual memory, sounds, and other senses and feelings helps you recall and apply what you learned. Nature and experience are out there—words guide us to make more connections between them.

So I will call them the audience, and you the presenter, because you have stepped into a role apart from this group, a role for which you are qualified in your special knowledge, in your outstanding ability to share your knowledge, and in your catalytic influence to promote the discovery of connections by others.

Progress can seem pitifully slow. You can know all the names of the possible mistakes. You can recite the rules that foster success, but find that the inertia of habit still controls your behavior. Don't give up. More knowledge will expand your resources, but your true power to make a difference comes from your honest feelings about yourself and your audience. Your abilities will grow to fill the one true boundary—the space defined by your respect for the subject and for your audience. Your constant work to improve is the deepest way to show this affection for your subject, your audience, and your time together.

> *When a superior person knows the causes which make instruction successful, and those which make it of no effect, they can become a teacher of others.*
>
> *Thus in one's teaching, one leads and does not drag; one strengthens and does not discourage; one opens the way but does not conduct to the end without the learner's own efforts.*
>
> *Leading and not dragging produces harmony.*
>
> *Strengthening and not discouraging makes attainment easy.*
>
> *Opening the way and not conducting to the end makes the learner thoughtful.*
>
> *One who produces such harmony, easy attainment, and thoughtfulness may be pronounced a skillful teacher.*
>
> attributed to Confucius

CHAPTER 2

THE CREATIVE PROCESS

If you were placed on trial for being creative,
what evidence of your guilt would the prosecution find?
David Campbell

I f there was one formula for the optimal presentation, one best way, then everybody would do it that way. That formula would become the dominant form and immediately become very familiar to us all, thus losing the essential element of novelty, and (assuming we're not talking about television) the formula would then cease to be the one best way. Success is so specific to the people, place, and time of the situation that there are a multitude of ways to succeed. What works with one crowd can kill you with another. Live, interactive communicators must create their way through every moment of their work.

Your job is to invent rewarding new experiences for your audience, to innovate ahead of their needs. Robert J. Sternberg compares creativity to the age-old advice given to investors, to buy low and sell high. Creative individuals are consistently able to buy an idea low—to see value in a new concept where no one else does—and then to hold on to it and cultivate it until they can sell it high as a useful item. The key words of his definition are *consistently*, *new*, and *useful*. Creative persons are not just lucky, they are consistently good at finding new ideas. These truly new ideas are not just oddities, they are valuable oddities that succeed in their niche.

Creativity is a mooshy-squooshy process, complex beyond linear dissection. Taking out the pieces and giving them names helps us understand how a frog works, but it also kills the proverbial frog. The typical image of creativity focuses on the moment of insight, the "ah-ha!" moment, Edison's one percent. But in the creative process, the approach that consistently gives us new and useful ideas, this moment of discovery is only the fourth step of a five-step process described by creativity researcher David Campbell:

1. the preparation phase

2. the concentration phase

3. the incubation phase

4. the insight, "ah-ha!" phase

5. the verification and testing phase

Many of us neglect the preparation and go right on to the "creative" part. Others never leave the preparation phase for fear of making the creative leaps. If you want to be consistently creative, you must take all five steps.

Preparation

The preparation phase is a long period of gathering all the resources needed to solve a problem. Some of this preparation will take place long before a presentation, some may happen in the few minutes just before you go on. Part of this preparation begins before  birth, in that it helps to be blessed with mental strength and agility to begin with. Children growing up with a healthy sense of self-esteem in an environment that respects and rewards their inventiveness should carry the habits of creativity into adulthood. It also helps if the adults surrounding the child are competent and effective in a variety of fields. This richly diverse environment encourages a multitude of interests from many disciplines that can bring new perspectives to solving problems. A person who has watched wildlife biologists study the ranges and feeding habits of brown bears using radio tracking devices might transfer these ideas to studying the movements of visitors within a theme park (minus the tranquilizer darts and ear tagging).

Curious, playful minds, always looking for new stimulation from diverse areas, must also have a strong foundation of knowledge within the field where they hope to create. It is easier to move ahead when you are already running at the front of the pack; otherwise, you run the risk of reinventing the familiar. But knowledge in the field can also keep you stuck in the same rut. That's partially why it also helps to be young: You don't know enough to know "it can't be done." Even so, knowledge in the field helps. More patents are granted to forty-five-year-olds than to fifteen-year-olds.

But these are not attributes that you can do very much about. Aside from fortunate birth, high energy, and broad interests, preparation is just the plain work of defining the problem and gathering information, and it is also the subject of the following chapter.

Concentration

The concentration phase of the creative process is that period of intense, obsessive wrestling with the problem once it is identified. This is the period when families, friends, and any other obligations are neglected as the creator struggles with the prob-  lem night and day. In this period, the dedication, the sense of destiny, the monomania of creators can make them a real pain to live or work with.

Here is where the energy and focus of the manic/depressive give them their costly advantage. The extreme highs of the manic phase fuel the bold leaps, the concentration, and the perseverance characteristic of the "artistic temperament." Many people, to varying degrees, have learned to harness the energy of manic states to help them accomplish tasks. Losing a night's sleep is one of the surest ways to push yourself toward the manic end of the scale. Watch the production crew and cast of a play as they move toward opening night to see strong-willed, nonconformist, artistic temperaments harnessed to accomplish a common goal. Watch also the drinking, smoking, and general turbulence that seem to come with the territory, and how the discipline of art brings order to the chaos of their lives.

Of course, just being disruptive or self-destructive does not mean a person is creative. Just as there are crabs that have learned to disguise themselves by attaching sponges and barnacles to their backs, some humans adopt caricature trappings of "the creative person." This gives them permission for self-indulgent behavior that actually produces little innovative output. In fact, within groups, they expend much of their energy stifling the creative output of others that might expose their own fraudulent nature. Fortunately for me, I have never run into anyone like this.

Incubation

All of this intensity eventually becomes counterproductive. Here is where you must get away from the problem. Archimedes was in the tub, Machiavelli was living on a farm, and Newton was resting under an apple tree when their insights dropped in on them. This means taking a vacation, reading  a book, chopping wood, getting some sleep, dropping the problem with disgust—whatever it is that enables you to let go of it for a while. Creative individuals become aware of this phase of the process and move into it with confidence knowing that they have to let go in order for another part of the brain to go to work.

Remember that in the arena of informal or recreational learning—in the "mind on vacation" business—this may be precisely what your audience is doing when they are with you. Allow your audience to engage in some creative reflection of their own. Everybody is working on their own set of projects and you can never know how they are using the stimulation that you offer.

Insight

Out of nowhere, then (it seems), comes that flash of insight. It may not be a practical answer, a reasonable answer, or a serious answer, but something connects. The answer may be outrageous, but it is the start of a negotiation that leads you in a new direction.

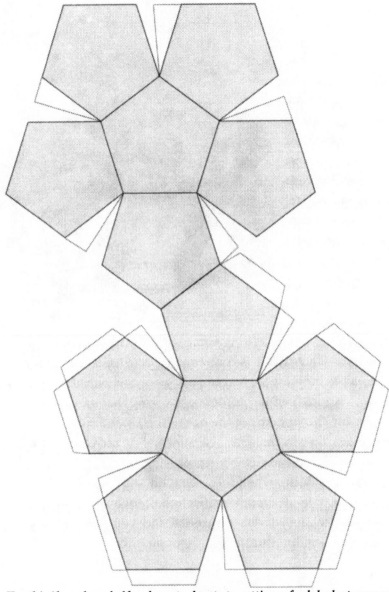

Try this if you have half an hour to devote to getting a fresh look at your subject (or if you just need a break).
Copy and enlarge this flattened-out dodecahedron. On each pentagon, write one of the facets of your subject. Cut out the entire shape and glue or tape the tabs together. Rolling the completed die will bring a different facet to the top. Look for new relationships through the body of the die as well as on the surface.
(Don't get caught.)

Much of the work in creativity enhancement involves mental tricks that can cycle the concentration and incubation phases more quickly in hopes of reaching the "ah-ha!" phase more often. Many of these techniques involve deliberately looking at the problem from another perspective. One common technique is seeking a metaphor for the problem. Abraham Lincoln was often "reminded of stories" as he wrestled with his incredible burdens. Another technique is to work backwards, imagining the problem as solved and then tracing the steps back to where you are now. Or, a problem can be turned on its head, by asking yourself what would you never, ever want to do in this case? What approach would give you the opposite of what you want? Your imagination helps distance you from information. Ask yourself how a problem would look from the point of view of someone from Mars, a dog, a mouse, or your grandmother—all mental tricks to help you gain new perspective.

Another strategy is to free more of your brain to seek insight. Externalize information, writing it down on cards that can be manipulated, rather than juggling things in your head. In the 1860s, long before storyboard developers began moving sticky-notes around on the wall, Russian chemist Mendeleyev made a card game of his quest for order that led to the familiar periodic table of the elements. As the song by Michael Offutt goes:

> *He wondered if Nature really had a master plan,*
> *If the elements had a pattern that one could understand,*
> *So he bought a bunch of cards and on each one wrote the name,*
> *Of an element and its weight, and then he played the game.*

We do the same process of externalizing information when we write the elements of our presentation or workshop on cards and then move them about on a board, experimenting with different arrangements. Many computer outlining programs will convert a linear outline into a tree chart that shows elements in a maplike fashion. You can also map your ideas onto three-dimensional surfaces. Try writing all the characters and aspects of a story on the surface of a beach ball with a marker pen. If you are going to tell the story of Edison's research laboratory, Edison would be the first name you wrote on the ball. But now include the workmen, Mrs. Edison, the dog, the mailman, the cat, lights, phonographs, mice, the boy who delivered sandwiches at noon—all written on the ball as they radiate out from the initial character. Normally the story would be told from the perspective of the central character, Edison. But now turn the ball so that a less obvious character is foremost. What perspective does that character have? What would this look like from Edison's critic's perspective? What would a winery tour look like from a grape's point of view? All of these creative games stir the pot in your search for the happy accident.

Testing

Finally, though, we have to taste the soup. Whereas before, you have resisted the urge to evaluate, now begins the process of testing the usefulness of the ideas. Even this phase requires the tolerance of ambiguity to realize that there may be many right answers to the problem. On a team, another person may have the task of "working out the details" of your great concept. Or you may have to shift mental gears to become the person adept at details and implementation. You may have to be the person who crumples the paper and says, "Back to the drawing board," or you may be the one who fishes the idea back out of the trash can and says, "Wait a minute, this gives me another idea." This is the time for constructive criticism from low-risk audiences, which builds on ideas and suggests ways to improve them. The contemporary image of creative teams involves flipcharts and facilitators, but consider this description by Max Hastings of the origin of the steel "rhino" tusks that allowed allied tanks to break through hedgerows in Normandy in 1944 rather than climbing up and exposing their underbellies to the deadly German *panzerfaust*.

> Every American armoured unit had been puzzling over the hedgerow problem, and one day Captain Jimmy de Pew of the 102nd summoned a "bull session" of his men to chew it over. A Tennessee hillbilly named Roberts asked slowly: "Why don't we get some saw teeth and put them on the front of the tanks and cut through these hedges?" The crowd of men roared with laughter. But Sergeant Culin, a notably shrewd soldier known in the unit both as a chess player and a man impatient of army routines, said "Hang on a minute, he's got an idea there."

It seems from this evidence that groups can come up with creative solutions without excessive attention to process, and even without dry-erase markers.

If the audience finds your communication both "original and good," then it is, by definition, creative. Your hard work and risk-taking have paid off. Savor your success, because a creative presentation is a series of calculated risks, and you get few "degree of difficulty" points for innovations that miss the mark by being too far out or too far ahead of their time. Creative acts are often destructive acts, and the creative process is often seen as disruptive and wasteful. Society rewards results, not self-indulgence.

Still, "If an idea isn't scary, it probably isn't an idea to begin with." It's just risk versus reward. Your audience is your investment partner, your fellow explorer, risking time and attention under your leadership. They want you to take them somewhere different—while remaining within certain boundaries. Due diligence requires you to judge where the audience boundaries lie at any given time, just as creative leadership requires you to constantly challenge and push at them.

He that will not apply new remedies must expect new evils;
for time is the greatest innovator;
and if time alters things to the worse,
and wisdom and counsel shall not alter them to the better,
what shall be the end?

Francis Bacon

CHAPTER 3
OBJECTIVES & INVESTIGATION

The main thing to consider is your purpose *in writing.* Why are you sitting down to write?
Dr. Rudolf Flesch

Because, sir, it is more comfortable than standing up.
E. B. White

As writer Anne Lamott put it, "If you want to make God laugh, just tell her your plans." This chapter looks at setting objectives and at the investigative phases of creative communication. Life is parallel, but books are serial, so I must present these steps in some sort of order, even though they are actually undertaken in a more mixed-up process. Hardly anyone works from such a formal plan, but the structure needs to sit somewhere in the back of your mind, attracting ideas into the right places as they present themselves.

Just as in building a house, a presentation has several stages of construction. The old expression "cut and dried" refers to the point where pieces of wood have been sawn and seasoned, and require only assembly. Felling the trees, clearing the site, and preparing the materials have already been accomplished. In communication, as in construction, you ask, where does your work come in and how far do you take it? Communication can be sliced into five overlapping phases: getting attention, maintaining interest, informing, persuading, and directing action. Your overall objective will consist of one or (usually) more of these five phases and we will examine each of them in the following chapters. Which of these phases you must complete depends upon where the audience is and where you want to lead them. If they are already paying attention to you, then you don't need to put energy into getting more attention. If your ultimate objective is to generate donations, votes or sales, then neglecting to direct action renders your other efforts pointless.

Consider two acts of communication. In the first instance you are selling kitchen knives at a flea market. In order to sell the knives you must:

(1) Get people to stop and pay attention to you,

(2) hold their interest while you

(3) inform them about the product, and

(4) persuade them to buy the product, and

(5) help them complete the purchase.

In the second case you are asked for directions to the nearest bathroom, and all you have to do is give direction. Informing the questioner about the role of bathrooms in history or persuading them that outhouses are actually healthier would be inappropriate. If someone asks you what time it is, you don't need to tell them how to build a watch.

Pure entertainment just needs to get attention and hold interest. At the other end of the spectrum, agitprop theater in the thirties (and again in the sixties) actually went beyond persuasiveness and tried to get the audience to take political action directly to the streets as soon as they emerged from the theater. Teachers might simply give information and direct action, or they might broaden their charge to developing interest and changing attitudes.

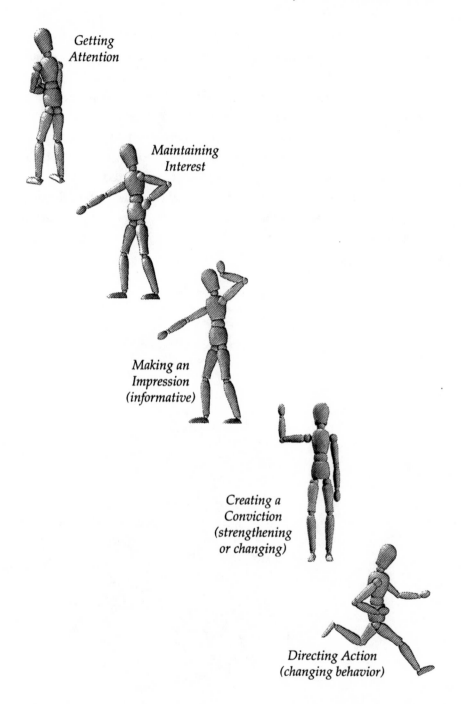

*Getting
Attention*

*Maintaining
Interest*

*Making an
Impression
(informative)*

*Creating a
Conviction
(strengthening
or changing)*

*Directing Action
(changing behavior)*

Communication may involve any or all of these five phases.

Deciding where you want to go will prevent wasted effort by making your goals clearer to both yourself and the audience. Objectives may change as you are under way, but a conscious shift is going to be more effective than aimless wandering. In a more expensive communication, such as an advertising campaign, you might devote a lot of time to defining your objective, writing it down as if it were from the audience's point of view. "The audience will develop a greater brand loyalty to Duff beer supported by an understanding of its brewing process." You may need to change destinations as you learn more about your fellow voyagers, but the journey begins with setting a realistic goal.

Is there a plan
— or shall I
just start
sawing?

Investigation, Inference & Invention
of Self, Subject & Audience

To bring value to your audience, you must know your stuff. To develop your range as a presenter, you must know yourself. To succeed with an audience, you must know as much as you can about them. Your research and preparation moves from investigation of facts, through inference about connections, to the invention and synthesis of the moment.

The facts you begin with may be statistical data about a group of people or they may be based on the senses, just as Sherlock Holmes used his powers of observation to note details of clothing and calluses on the hands. Much may prove irrelevant as you move forward, but you don't know that now.

Gather all the facts, then move on to the later stages. What are the logical and practical implications of the facts? Here we enter the danger zone: The list of inference errors is a long and bloody one, so stick your toe in the water before you jump.

Finally, invention. If the details are not there, you must create them. For any experience to be interesting it must be absolutely specific and detailed. Choose the color, the number, how damp the ground was, how she felt about her new car, how the dog smelled, what their ride from the airport was like. Even when the details are obviously not factual, they give the audience the essential taste of truth. Anything generalized is lifeless. Still, invention with the subject is so dangerous that we have built special boundaries, the realm of fiction, to contain it. These boundaries between fact and fiction are agreements with your audience. Violate these agreements, violate this trust, and they will reject you.

Your Subject

There is no substitute for the palpable depth of knowledge that allows you to reward the curiosity of your audience. Depth is found in coherent, connected detail ferreted out by research and experience. There are performance reasons to know your subject completely as well. You won't tire as easily when you know your subject. Working at tasks you have mastered requires less glucose in the brain than those where you are uncertain. You also have to be totally prepared so you can deal with the unexpected. The variables created by the audience will give you enough to think about.

Still, we can infer many different things from the same set of facts, and it may be that this defines the work of the thoughtful presenter. The job is often to be helpfully "other minded." Whatever conclusion we reach, we must point out other, equally valid conclusions and explore what caused us to think as we did. As Laurent Daloz wrote, "Mentors toss little bits of disturbing information in their students' paths, little facts and observations, insights and perceptions, theories and interpretations—cow plops on the road to truth."

Making inferences is thinking. Sometimes we shift the work of inference to the audience members by providing direct experience. At our open-air living history museum, we were frustrated by the often facile conclusions visitors would make about how hard/easy it was to "live back then." To give them more evidence, we placed as many opportunities for hands-on experiences within reach as possible, such as a two-man crosscut saw resting in its kerf halfway through a log. Parents and their children would start sawing the log and express their conclusions stimulated by their experience. If they said, "Boy, that was hard!" we would offer that they were just not used to it and that after they built up the muscles it would be a lot easier. If they said, "Boy, that was easy!" we'd say that perhaps after having to do this for hours every day they might welcome less strenuous and repetitious work. Our goal was not to invalidate their personal construction of meaning, but to remind them that it *is* constructed. They thought once, they thought again—not bad for a few minutes' work, considering we could have just told them that it was hard/easy to cut wood in the old days. The audience has work to do. See that they do it.

Your Subject	Yourself	Your Audience

INVESTIGATION

Know your stuff. How does your subject innovate or adapt? Who makes the rules? How have other people described it? Who are its friends? How much diversity is present? What are the boundaries? What does it need to survive? How much tolerance is there for deviation? What crises has it faced in the past? (And every other question that you can imagine.)

Know yourself. You need versatility on both the inside and the outside to succeed as a presenter. Awareness of your prejudices will help you to shift your point of view to see things as others do. What were the values of your education? Are there aspects of your appearance or voice that upstage your message? Ask for honest feedback and use it.

Know your audience. First, know all you can about people in general. Then, specifically: what about your audience and individuals within it? Where are they from? What is their education level? What are their current concerns? Who are their heroes, their enemies? What are their expectations? Are they bored, tired, angry, excited, upbeat, fearful, happy, confused?

INFERENCE

What connections can you infer between the facts of your subject? More importantly, what can you lead the audience to infer from the facts, and what does their inference reveal about themselves?

How might the facts discovered through your investigation of your own background shape your character? Your conclusions implied by the facts may be wrong, but the point is to maintain an edifying discourse with yourself.

If you find out that the audience has already endured four hours of lectures, you might reasonably infer that they would like a change of pace. Check for assumptions and biases that might lead you to make an incorrect inference.

INVENTION

All of these divisions among subject, self, and audience dissolve as
your audience becomes the subject, as you become the audience
watching them engage with the subject. Synthesis happens.
We invent ourselves every minute in a shared
experience with the audience. Real life
is made up of specific details,
nuance, and the
rightness of
now.

Critical Reflection on Yourself

Somewhere between the myth of objectivity and the dismissal of ourselves as mindless puppets of some interest group lies an honest investigation of the assumptions that guide our thinking. Critical reflection is the intellectual habit of relentlessly uprooting the commonsense assumptions that disguise power relationships and distort our projections of reality. If your parents exhibited strong prejudices regarding race and gender, how might it affect your thinking? How has your cultural environment shaped your habitual perceptions? Awareness of these biases and their cultural origins leaves your mind free to deal honestly with the subject. This habit of questioning makes our communication more inclusive, more diverse, less old-hat, and models for others the good habits of democratic dialog. Getting out of the rut that you have been in gives you a new and broader view—yet another way of stepping out from the center of the universe.

None of this is easy or comfortable. Stephen Brookfield likens the experience of losing our comfortable foundations of assumptions to that of Wile E. Coyote when he chases Roadrunner out over the edge of a cliff. As long as he remains unaware of his situation, he defies gravity and remains suspended in space. But one beat after he looks down, and realizes that there is nothing beneath him, the laws of physics reengage and he plummets to the canyon floor. Perhaps if Coyote never looked down, he would never fall. But if he does not look down of his own accord, there will inevitably come a "Bee–beep!" and a pointing foot from Roadrunner. The fall is just as long and made harder by Roadrunner's gloat.

A warning, though: Introspection and relativism are unwelcome habits among those who need a more certain worldview. In any case, this is just background—your audience might not be that interested in the forces that have shaped you. Subtext is subtext. Don't bore your audience with your life story or alienate them with your insights into the inauthenticity of their own beliefs. You're better off knowing, but the audience may well thank you for not sharing.

Your Audience

In *A Midsummer Night's Dream*, Shakespeare presents as comedy a mistaken inference, a gross underestimation of the intelligence of the audience. (Something that we lesser mortals experience more often as tragedy.) Shakespeare shows some clueless "rude mechanics" rehearsing *Pyramus and Thisby*, the play within the play, that they plan to present to the ladies and gentlemen of the court. In the following exchange, they worry about the shocking effect of their presentation on the audience, and devise a plan.

Bottom   There are things in this comedy of *Pyramus and Thisby* that will never please. First, Pyramus must draw a sword to kill himself; which the ladies cannot abide.

Starveling I believe we must leave the killing out, when all is done.

Bottom   Not a whit: I have a device to make all well. Write me a prologue; and let the prologue seem to say, we will do no harm with our swords, and that Pyramus is not kill'd indeed; and, for the more better assurance, tell them that I Pyramus am not Pyramus, but Bottom the Weaver: this will put them out of fear.

They also make a point of having the lion say that he is not a real lion, and constantly beg the audience not to be frightened. As a result the ladies and gentlemen of the court think that the rude mechanics are idiots and ridicule them throughout their presentation.

As a more skillful mechanic, you must check your assumptions about your audience. The more you know, the more precisely you can target your goals and correctly interpret feedback. This is not so much planning as it is deliberately shifting your point of view to become the master of a situation rather than its victim. Approaching or delivering a presentation from a purely egocentric point of view rarely succeeds, but the more egocentric the presenter, the less likely they are to be aware of their failure.

So what are the audience's expectations? Do as the African proverb states, "Never check the depth of a river with both feet." Ask lots of questions before you go in. "Am I right in assuming that . . ." is a good way to check your inferences as well as to make a connection with the audience. Your promotion people can sometimes create confusion and disappointment by promising the audience something other than what you planned. Ask your audience what their expectations are before you reveal the contents. You may need to make some rapid revisions.

"Icebreaker" activities help at this stage by generating small talk and flushing out personalities to reveal potential misunderstandings and opportunities. This is a standard practice in participatory television programs. Before the broadcast begins, the warm-up man plays games with the audience, offering prizes and interacting to see whom to choose and whom to avoid for the main event.

Most after-dinner speaking experts advise you to take advantage of any preprandial mixer events to glean knowledge of the audience. This is great if mixers don't make you nervous and tempt you to drink. If they do, make a courtesy appearance and then disappear. There are those who can face a huge audience with poise and aplomb if they have not made wrecks of themselves at the mixer beforehand. You'll usually find me hiding in the kitchen.

The more time you can devote to investigating the audience the more likely you are to make correct inferences about how to reach them. Target your starting point to the background of the audience and the development of the content to their intellectual capacity. An audience of experts with long experience in a given field will more

What are you dodging for?
They couldn't hit an elephant
at this dist....

Last words of General
John B Sedgewick, 1864

easily see the larger patterns than novices. Experts will quickly recognize concepts holistically using the right side of the brain, whereas novices need a left-brained, sequential, spelling-it-out style.

Usually, you will face an audience that is ready to go along with you, but sometimes you want to incite a more critical audience—one that will contribute more to the exploration of an issue. Other times you will encounter an indifferent or resistant audience. You will need to find some common ground from which you can begin to reorient these audiences before you can proceed.

If your audience seems indifferent, find out why. Are they there by choice? Have they just endured a miserably boring presentation before getting to you? Even if the presentations before yours weren't so bad, they may be just worn out from the sheer quantity of material. The environment may make it hard for them to see or hear. In such a situation you need to get attention and crank up your strategies to maintain interest.

Sometimes you will face an audience with whom you share too much common ground, whose knowledge of the subject is just as profound as yours. They may perceive you as having nothing new to offer, or as not understanding the subject as well as they do. If this is what you're up against, you are better off knowing it in advance so that you can develop your new facts and ideas on a base that acknowledges their preexisting ones.

Toughest of all, you may walk into a hostile audience. You may represent the enemy in some way, or the audience may perceive a hidden agenda of some sort. Where change is perceived, fear won't be far away. Your race or religion, politics or looks may represent a threat. Even if you are relatively close to the audience's point of view, the proximal enemy may be attacked more viciously than the distant one. Knowing this in advance helps you choose an idea development pattern better suited to the hostile audience, such as problem-solving, where you work together toward solution.

Obviously, there are certain circumstances where you can find more specific information about your audience. If you find out that your audience consists largely of lawyers, you can make some logical inferences about how they might reason, their income level, and their interests in contemporary issues. You can, of course, make embarrassing errors. You may have only rough statistical data. Sometimes you just have the look in their eyes. Still, you must find out as much as you can. You have to ask. You have to look.

Audience Expectations According to Scale

Audiences usually have reasonable expectations for your tradeoff between "polish" and responsiveness. In face-to-face, spontaneous communication, we expect nonfluencies, such as hesitations or repetitions, but we also expect immediate responsiveness. When we encounter someone who does not seem to be in the moment with us we might call them "human tape recorders"—they have given the same explanation, made the same sales pitch, presented the same lecture so many times that we and they are alienated by their boredom. On the other hand, when reading a book or watching a movie, or sitting in a large audience, we expect a well-crafted presentation that delivers engagingly structured changes. We don't expect a novel or a play to respond to us, but we don't expect sloppiness either. From the audience's point of view, the less they have input and responsiveness, the more they expect you to get your act together.

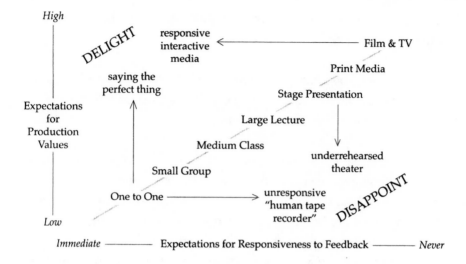

Deviation from the range of reasonable expectations can delight or disappoint.

When your work diverges from expectations, you can either delight or disappoint. Saying just the right thing in the right way at the right time is considered very intelligent and attractive. New interactive media that allow you to follow your own interests are also an unexpected treat.

Diverging from expectations in the other direction disappoints audiences. What torture it is to endure a poorly paced, rambling presentation where you cannot ask questions, explore your own interests, or even escape. At least with a book, you are not reading the first draft, nor the second. Other intelligent readers and editors have done their best to make your experience as profitable as possible. What's more, if it fails to deliver, you can put it down without anyone knowing. Not so with presentations.

Another significant variation in media / audience size is the number of sensory channels available. Most all of the information is going to come in through your eyes and ears. The two senses work together to cross-check and confirm information as your brain makes recognizable wholes. Touch, taste, and smell are more available when the proximity to the audience is greater. They are thus rare treats and lead to a primary law of responsible communication, a law that I remember as *Habeas Corpus*.

> *When people have gone to the trouble to bring their bodies to you, you must do everything that you can to take advantage of their physical presence.*

When you have an audience in close proximity to a resource, be sure that you exhaust every direct sensory experience first. Let them explore and discover the resource before you begin taking their time on things that are better derived from a book. Can they smell it at home? No? Then let them smell it here. Can they discover it for themselves at home? No? Then let them discover it here. They have come all this distance; don't substitute symbolic words for the richer experience. Don't tell them about it—let them do it!

Sometimes the sensory problem is in a bad translation from one medium to another. A witty newspaper column read on the radio does not take full advantage of radio's ability to use location sound and the actual voices of the participants to bring us to the location. The lack of richness fails to meet our expectations. Conversely, transcribing a perfectly satisfying radio program into print will often produce disappointing reading. Audiences are entitled to expect every medium to be used to its fullest advantage.

Feedback & Constant Invention

Investigation, inference, and invention never stop. They just cycle faster to guide the changes at every moment of the presentation as you negotiate the most rewarding path. The process of conversational presentation is very similar to the way we walk, repeatedly falling forward and catching ourselves. We constantly adjust our pace and step to adapt to the terrain. We don't plan every step, we just look ahead and choose the best path. With a heavy load we must go slower; if we go fast we cast off excess baggage. In the same way, we can leave people behind. We ask, "Are you with me?" "Let me help you catch up." "Oh, I'm way ahead of you." A *faux pas* is a false step. We say, "Don't go there!" We make a leap of faith. We might be faulted for rambling on, for being pedestrian, or for constantly tripping people up.

The sequence of steps is a journey; the sequence of observations and connections is a story. It is no wonder that the earliest and still the most common form of story is a journey, describing the adventures to get to a certain place. The series of steps that lead to a destination take on a meaningful whole for the listener. Your competency in presentation is also founded on a sensitive response to the environment—paying attention to the social terrain and having a wide variety of steps to call upon. The more communication skills you have, the better you will be able to adapt to precisely fit the circumstances.

As in any journey, it's handy to occasionally climb a tree to see how you've been doing and what lies ahead. Before and during your presentation, practice shifts of consciousness by imagining the event from the perspective of the audience as well as imagining a synoptic, God's-eye view of the presentation, seeing the whole of the unfolding event. During the presentation you must scramble up these imaginary trees while staying tuned in to the moment-by-moment details. Trusted informants can give you quick feedback during breaks. Be ready to adapt. General Dwight D. Eisenhower often observed that "plans are everything before a battle, and nothing once it begins."

Analyze audience feedback—objectively evaluating the meaning of their responses (remembering that you may be wrong). The audience response will give you the clues when you need to change. You must be ready to make the change rather than expecting the audience to adapt to your misjudgment. Because of the relationship between the subject and the audience, you may need to put more or less energy into maintaining interest. Sometimes you don't call the sequence correctly and find that you need to add or subtract steps.

Respond when necessary, but don't let the feedback throw you off from your intention. Psychologist, writer, and teacher B. F. Skinner wrote about how he was conditioned by audience response. "I once gave what was supposed to be the same lecture to fifteen audiences. I used a good many slides that served as an outline, but I began to abbreviate or drop comments that did not seem to arouse interest and retain everything that brought a clean-cut response or a laugh. Near the end of the series, I had to struggle to say anything worthwhile."

I would wager that it was Skinner's audience that was struggling near the beginning of the lecture series. Following the arc of all endeavor, Skinner probably reached his peak combination of challenge and support somewhere between one-half and two-thirds of the way through the series before the seduction of immediate gratification drove the more challenging ideas from the stage.

Sensitivity to the nuances of feedback is double-edged in another way. It helps you adjust to your audience, but it can make you too responsive to the negative. You can be too hard on yourself and become frightened of feedback and never venture from your accustomed forms. This would reduce your chance of failure but also ensure that you never grow.

This can be a hard business. As you improve, savor your successes; put them in a bank against the inevitable setbacks. Remember, this is a craft. Every presentation, every performance, is just something you made, something for you to learn from. What kind of pottery would you make if you judged your pots only by how you felt when you made them, but never risked actually evaluating them from the users' perspective when you were done?

I threw him the decoys. . . . They didn't look very much like ducks to me. I told him so. He was pretty short when he answered me.

"They look like ducks to a duck," he said. "Trouble with most people is that they always think about everything selfish. You ain't going duck hunting to shoot you. You're going to shoot ducks. From up in the sky the things will look like ducks to a duck."

The Old Man and the Boy, Robert Ruark

Chapter 4

Attention, Distractions & Rapport

Actually, I even took off my shoe and pounded on the desk.
Nehru said that I shouldn't have used such an unparliamentary method.
It became a widely publicized incident which outraged the sensibilities
of many Westerners.

Nikita Khrushchev

Soviet Premier Khrushchev regretted his shoe-pounding episode at the United Nations. It got him the attention that he wanted, but it started him off on the wrong foot. The attention-getting phase of communication is the most primitive. A lightning bolt and crash of thunder will get your attention, as will the roar of a mountain lion. A baby cries to get attention. A person dresses in a shocking manner to get attention. "Headless Body in Topless Bar" shouts the tabloid. "Is your telephone giving you cancer? Answers at eleven!" teases the television. Their information content is not complex, but they get your attention, and get things started.

Attention requires energy and will swing like a compass needle to the source of greatest stimulation. Because you are usually new to the audience, you have their attention right at the start and can build from there. The desired end determines the best beginning, so your attention-getter should support the rest of your message. Hitler walks alone down the aisle of ranked troops and communicates his message as the single leader of the state. A minister in vestments climbs to the pulpit, a clown enters in a tiny automobile: All say

"Pay attention to me now, I am what is different, I am what is important, and you already have my first message."

The essence of attention is **contrast**. Somehow you stand out from the background; either externally as perceived by the senses of the audience, or internally as based on prior knowledge. This contrast is often more effective when it is a qualitative difference, not quantitative. The musical ringing of tapping on a glass cuts through the din of conversation better than shouting. In a world that shouts, quiet dignity may get attention. Standing up works only if everyone else is seated. Moving works only if everyone else is motionless. Postures and positions that make you bigger communicate dominance. That's why the park ranger wears a big hat and stands atop a stump. So find or create the visual focal point—a stairway, an arch—to emphasize your contrasting role as a leader.

Attention-getting may begin with the publicity for your event so the audience is prefocused on you. If you are already known to the audience, you have the advantage of internal contrast with them—you attract attention because you stand out in their minds. This can work against you as well. If you are well known, you may carry a baggage of expectations that distracts from your current objective, but at least it gets your foot in the door.

Sometimes focusing attention is just a matter of employing simple mechanics with the audience. To get them pointed in the right direction you have them gather in a special place where all the seats face an elevated platform for the speaker. Their attention is focused by the event and the place. Rituals are another way of focusing attention. "All rise" when the judge enters the courtroom is not just a show of respect, it is a physical activity that orients the group's attention. Applause, singing together, sharing food, laughing at a shared joke, competing for a prize—all direct attention of the audience away from private conversations and into the shared experience.

In an informal setting, you may need more aggressive tactics to focus attention. Wearing a costume or uniform, speaking loud, looking good—all draw the crowd, focus their attention on you, and get the ball rolling. Ron Popeil, our "salesman of the century," had to turn passersby into an audience when he began hawking kitchen gadgets at state fairs. First, he would secure a location near the ladies' rest room to ensure that he would have plenty of traffic all day. Then with his jokes, give-aways, and demonstrations he would build up a crowd that in turn drew more of a crowd so he could get on to the business of selling.

The overt instruction from an introducer also tells our audience to pay attention to us. They build our credibility, share a personal insight about us, and articulate the importance of the presentation. A good introduction gives the audience just enough information and emotional setup so that both they and you can do your work without excessive confusion or distraction.

Some tension works in your favor. We want to

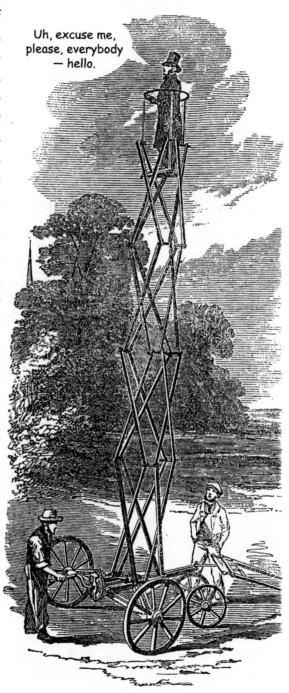

43

Relabel and rechannel any anxiety you might feel into enthusiasm and excitement about meeting and sharing with new people.

live in a predictable world and understand why people behave the way they do. A person whose behavior does not match our expectations is bound to be interesting. What were their motives? Why did they behave other than I would? If the audience learns that you are unusual in some manner—having endured a serious experience or behaved in some unusual way—they will pay more attention to you. Knowledge of strange people and events could be useful later on. We pay attention to this unusual behavior and try to integrate it with our bank of experience. That's what the audience is trying to do with you.

Always, though, remember the paradox of attention. If you hold the audience's attention constantly, they get little from the encounter. When will they have time to do their work? They need some time to reflect, to discuss, to "make meaning" from all of this new input. If you do not give them time, they will take it for themselves.

Allow time for discussion and reflection, either allocating specific time or accepting that your audience will slip in and out of their state of attention to do the work that they have to do. As brain-based learning expert Eric Jensen wrote, "You can either have your learner's attention or they can be making meaning, but never both at the same time. Cramming more content per minute, or moving from one piece of learning to the next, virtually guarantees that little will be learned or retained."

Energy & Enthusiasm

No matter where you are, energy is a constant element of capturing and holding attention. Energy makes you stand out from the crowd and command attention. No one can observe top communicators without being impressed with the energy and power they direct into their work. You must show that what you're doing is interesting and exciting—the easiest way to do that is when it really is. When you really like what you do, you can be expansive about it, and that communicates infectious enthusiasm and draws attention. If the spark is not there, then it costs you. If you don't have any energy, they don't feed you back any energy.

You can draw energy both from your enthusiasm for the subject and for the audience, and even from whatever normal tension you feel. Channel any apprehension into the excitement of meeting new people and the excitement of success. Enthusiasm is infectious. To expose you to the germ, here are two experienced presenters talking about their enthusiasm for the audience.

> "It's the most wonderful feeling. When it's really clicking, when it's really happening, when they're really relating and responding, when the people are into it—it's just a roll, and the positiveness of the entire experience just feeds and feeds. It's just a pump all the way through. It pumps them up, it pumps you up. It's a back and forth exchange of the energy, rather

than having the energy sapped out of you because you've got bricks standing in front of you, or because you're the brick."

Christy Coleman

"There's a sense of constant focus in what you're doing and that time is not passing. And when you're talking to people, and you care about them, and things are working just the way they should, then every moment you listen becomes important, everything you say has a weight to it—not that it's important to the world, but that it's important at that moment. You'll suddenly stop and you'll look at all these people and they're looking at you like this is just great! And you didn't even know any of this, I mean, you're just talking to these people, and all of a sudden you see that you've been completely sharing something, and there was no time or anything between you, and that's a great time."

Marcus Hansen

It's no surprise that the origin of the word "enthusiasm" is the Greek *en + theos*, to be inspired by a god.

Orientation Eliminates Distractions

Orientation means getting your audience pointed in the right direction as soon as possible so that all of your energy can go into building momentum. You have their attention; now you inform the audience about the presentation and its value to them. Make a strong entrance and set your direction. Work to strengthen the attitudes that help you further your case and weaken those that work against you, removing obstacles and clearing the way. Your intention may be to entertain, to inform, or to persuade—but let them know. (Old friend Robert Watson, teaching historic site visitors about slavery,

begins with "Gather round everybody. We're going to do some learning together.") Presentations may need to move from stage to stage, first to inform, then to persuade, then to direct action. Each of these stages may need a reorientation. It might begin with "I'm going to show you how this works, show some example applications, and then let you come up and try it for yourself." Set up expectations and then proceed to meet them.

We can pay attention to only a very limited number of things at the same time, so we make constant, conscious decisions to determine what is signal and what is noise. What we call listening is actually selective hearing. We may even choose to process internal signals (daydream) if the external signals fail to interest. At a party we are often listening to one person and just monitoring the noise around us. But suddenly our monitoring system picks up words that capture our interest. The person who is speaking to us suddenly becomes the source of noise and we actively process only the signals coming in from the more interesting conversation next to us. We are distracted.

Distractions, like attention, can arise from inside as well as outside the heads of the audience. Your work shouldn't have to compete with lawn mowers, bus engines, or noisy projectors. Nor should you have to compete with people's drive to satisfy their frustrated intelligence. Much of the work of the introduction and your beginning is to reduce uncertainties that may potentially distract the audience. Tell the audience of your requirements so there will be no unproductive surprises. Reward the part of the audience's intelligence that tries to plan ahead. Satisfy the part of their mind that wants to know—"What is the game here? What are the rules? How long will this last? Will I have a chance to get an autograph, buy a can opener, see the gun fired, let my kid try it? Can I ask questions?" Not giving the audience this information at the start leaves these issues unresolved, nagging, and distracting.

Part of your work is the most subtle management of perception. The classic Maine guide in the 1940s always carried a revolver and a knife in his belt—not that he would ever place his clients in actual danger—but the *perception* of adventure and danger was essential to the client's pleasure. Looking the part of the professor, the wilderness guide, or the high-powered attorney—like all the requisite management of perception—can be viewed as cynical manipulation, or just the recognition of the economy of human attention. Meeting expectations in one arena leaves the audience's mental powers to concentrate on the real subject—not the irrelevant weirdness, but the important newness.

Just as you want to be the item of contrast in order to gain attention, you may need to reduce the contrast of other items. Look around and eliminate things that are out of context from both the visual and the aural sphere. You not only have to get away from the idling bus engine, or make them shut down the air compressor, you also have to eliminate your own distracting mannerisms. Don't let your appearance or vocal characteristics upstage you. Even your attention-getters can be distracting once their work is done. Repeated, mechanistic behaviors, mannerisms that would be amusing in a comic context, are deadly in any other. One consultant we hired had the habit

*Repetitious mannerisms
can be as distracting as
they are boring.*

of making lisping "tch" sounds when he wanted to interrupt a discussion with pronouncements that always began with "Frankly..."
To imitate him, all anyone had to do was go "Tch... Frankly..."
Such mechanical, repetitive behavior is more understandable, but
no less destructive, in persons giving repeat performances. I once
encountered a bored tour guide who began her spiel in every room
of a mansion with the formula: "This is the _____ room. We like to
call it the _____ room because of the _____s that cover the walls."
There was the rose room, the butterfly room, the daisy room, the
walnut room, and a half dozen more. Mispronouncing words, rock-
ing back and forth, formulaic transitions—countless mannerisms
await the chance to occupy the forefront of attention, not only distracting the audience, but stealing time away from more interesting
and creative behaviors. Attention, like a curious child, will wander
away if you leave it unoccupied. Cut all repetitive, useless filler from
your presentation and keep up the pace. Pauses should have a purpose, with work for the audience to do. If you are showing slides,

don't look at the screen and preface every image by saying "Now, this is a slide of . . ." Your audience *knows* it's a slide, you don't have to tell them. Such boring holes will leave desperate minds looking for something to do.

Choose the battles that you can win. In demonstrating early technology, I learned long ago never to work within 50 feet of a horse or a working blacksmith. You can't compete with big brown eyes or hammering and sparks. Any new activity is also going to be more interesting for a time than what you have to say. If the competition for attention is relevant to your subject, then use it to your best advantage. If you are talking about environmental changes, then a honking flight of geese overhead is a gift, not a distraction. When the distraction is a real interruption, and can't be used, then jump to one of the lower functions such as moving to the next location, or calling for a break. Still, short of injury to the audience, the show must go on somehow. The professional difference is the creative ability to turn a negative into a positive.

Sometimes the distraction can just take over. I once gave a slide-lecture on early American carpentry to an antique tool collectors' club. We gathered in half of a hotel meeting room that was divided by a thin folding partition. The other half was in use for a meeting of Mary Kay cosmetics saleswomen. Our two meetings coexisted until the Mary Kay ladies began announcing sales contest winners, and I had to slip my words between the cheers and applause that were erupting with increasing frequency. But then the singing began. Soon, all the women were on their feet singing to the tune of the "Battle Hymn of the Republic," "Mar-y, Mar-y Kay for-e-ver! Mar-y, Mar-y Kay for-e-ver!" The partition was shuddering from their ardor. Now there were no gaps for me to pop a word into. One of us could have gone over and asked them to hold it down, but it would have been like interfering with a religious service.

Some of my audience looked stricken, some were laughing at my predicament. If anyone was saying anything, I could not hear it. I started moving with the rhythm of the singing women, looked at the slide, and began to sing, to the tune of "Row, Row, Row Your

Basic human needs take priority over your message.

Boat," "Swing, swing, swing the axe, sharply down the log. Carefully, carefully, carefully, carefully, spike it with the dog!" Only the first few rows could hear me, but they joined in at full voice on the repeat so that the back of the audience was able to hear. We carried on like this from slide to slide to complete the program with all of us belting out the improvised verses. We stopped with great laughter and applause, but as we quieted down we realized there was now total silence from our neighbors. I brought up the lights and there, in the back door, was a group of pink-clad ladies staring in at us.

The needs of the audience change with the culture. Old Laurel and Hardy comedies seem horribly slow-paced today, as they labor to include every step and detail of the visual story. Over the years, we have learned the shortcuts of the cinematic language and move much faster. Comedians once used segues to move from one joke to another. ("Speaking of borscht, did you hear about . . .") Now the segue is gone. A transition in a presentation moves faster too. You don't want to leave your audience confused, but you don't need to spoon-feed them either. The trend is to trust the audience to make the connections with a minimum amount of cueing that something is about to change.

Basic Human Needs

Often, though, it is the most basic things that distract your audience. In 1954, humanist psychologist Abraham Maslow defined five basic human needs that we all try to satisfy in priority order. These five needs are: physiological, safety, belonging, self-esteem, and finally, self-actualization. You simply have to ensure that people feel safe and have had enough to eat, for example, before you can help them take many steps in their personal journey of self-actualization.

Maslow's hierarchy of human needs is the external reflection of the three-part structure of our brain, which is itself the echo of our evolutionary journey from our primitive vertebrate ancestors. The three parts are the reptilian brain, the limbic system, and the neocortex, symbolized by the image of the dragon, St. George, and the maiden.

The primitive dragon, or reptilian, brain takes care of survival through maintenance, territoriality, dominance, and mating behaviors. It's the part of you and your audience that has the intelligence level of a bunch of crocodiles. Its unchanging nature helps us survive, but, again, it makes us behave like a bunch of crocodiles.

Keeping the dragon brain under control is the limbic system, which I will choose St. George and the horse to represent. The limbic system evolved later in mammals, and has enough consciousness to express emotions such as aggression, fear, and affection, which, primitive though they seem, are a step up from the robotic, ritualized, reflexive, "cold-blooded" response of the dragon brain. The limbic system also helps us learn, as it is central to making memories of feelings and locations.

The largest portion of the human brain is the neocortex, or new, brain, symbolized by the maiden. This is the uniquely human area that talks and listens, reads and writes, designs and builds, and can

Our three-part, or triune, brain is composed of the reptilian, the emotional limbic system, and the most recently evolved neocortex.

creatively and logically think ahead. The neocortex has conscious control and can do so many wonderful things—including having dialogs with the other parts of the brain. Imagine you're at a meeting where your dragon brain says, "I'm hungry, let's go eat something." The limbic system says, "No, we can't be rude to our friends by leaving." The neocortex works on the problem and comes up with the best possible excuse to leave the meeting that will satisfy immediate survival needs as well as the longer-term social needs of the future. Between the three of them, they may come up with a way to avoid the situation in the future, such as remembering to snag a bite before the next meeting. Without the dragon brain you couldn't survive, without the limbic system you couldn't feel and remember, without the neocortex you wouldn't be able to read this book. They need each other and they influence each other. Your highly evolved ability to interpret something like written erotica will stimulate a limbic response, not to mention some basic physical responses that even crocodiles have proven highly successful at. More useful in our context, you can learn to control basic responses, such as fear of speaking, through changing the way you think about them in the neocortex. The dragon can be controlled.

Back to Maslow's hierarchy of needs. Taking them in order of importance, you will see how the basic animal needs must be met before the audience can devote attention to your more refined offerings.

1. Tend to physiological needs.

An overheated person who needs to use the bathroom is not going to pay attention to you. They will be looking for a drinking fountain or a bathroom or a place to sit down. If they have already been sitting for two hours when you begin, you can bet that physiological needs will take priority over your edifying commentary. See that the audience is cared for first. Check on the welfare of the group at regular intervals and at the first sign of need. Give them ten minutes out of each hour to get up and move around or talk with one another. One of the most well-intentioned but common failures is to give the audience too much material and not enough breaks. The brain can take in no more than the butt can endure.

2. Eliminate safety concerns.

No one can learn if they are seriously worried about threats to their selves, loved ones, or property. Someone who is worried about their car being broken into or if their children are safe with the baby-sitter will not be able to pay attention. If rush hour or an ice storm is approaching, your audience's minds will be occupied with poten-

Threats to personal safety tend to dominate your consciousness.

tial dangers on the highway, not with your content. Assure the audience that you will end early (and then do end early) because of the threat so they will be free to concentrate.

Nor should you pose a threat with your presentation. I once gave a demonstration of squaring a log with an axe at a genteel historical society meeting in a genteel southern coastal town. Part of my "act" was that chunks of wood would fly off, giving me the opportunity to say, "We just let the chips . . ." and then the audience would complete the phrase and get a laugh. This always worked well when I was outside on the grass at the same level as the audience. But this time I was on stage, elevated so that my feet were level with the faces of the audience. The audience was getting sprayed with small chips and I began the setup for the "Let the chips . . ." gag, when I popped loose a dinner plate–sized chunk of wood that flew out into the middle of the audience and struck a lady right flat in the face, quite hard. Idiotically, I continued with the joke and kept on going. It was a horrible moment, but I kept on, the audience aghast at how uncaring and callous I was, and concerned that they might be the next victims. I should have stopped and ensured that she was all

People go places to be together.

right before going on. Safety and good feelings, if not simple human compassion, come before content. The "show must go on" maxim applies only when the professionals are hurt, not the audience.

3. Strengthen feelings of belonging.

People go places and do things to be together. Learning follows well after the desire to have a shared experience and strengthen bonds with their family or extended social group. The need to belong with a group is more important than anything you might have to say. When Garrison Keillor announces a break in his two-hour radio program he sometimes says, "We're going to give the audience a chance to move around and see who else is here." Personal, emotional needs often supersede the exchange of ideas. Alienating members of the audience with hostile allusions and self-serving comments will override any fascinating content. One slip is all it takes and minds are off.

On a tour of an 1812-era Canadian fort, my guide, dressed as a soldier of the period, conducted his tour with textbook-proper technique of involvement and humor, yet the audience held back throughout his tour with distant tension. His jokes fell flat and his questions went unanswered. Why? He began the tour by asking if there were any Americans in the group. A few raised their hands. He walked over and said, "Oh well, then I'll have to keep an eye on you, and report you if I catch you spying so you can be arrested, because the whole point of this fort is to kill invading Americans." Although this was perhaps historically informative, what came through was his personal, present-day hostility toward Americans. Thus he began by alienating the Americans in the group, and embarrassing the other nationals who wondered when it might be their turn. He followed this with a presentation that depended on trust and rapport and wondered why folks are so unresponsive these days.

You must work to strengthen feelings of belonging. He could have easily begun by making us all honorary Canadians, and characterizing Americans as the aggressive nation to the south. You want to begin by bringing your audience closer, not by driving them away.

Getting people from groups that have already developed a structure, such as office coworkers or teenagers in school groups, to participate in hands-on activities is often very difficult. They have their own social dynamics that are more important than complying with your wishes. But again, you can engage their own social dynamics in focusing interest through this "take me to your leader" approach. Upon meeting the group, ask, "Who is the best *<insert your task here>* in your group?" They will shove forward their champion, their alpha, to try the task in question: reading, steering, cutting, whatever. You have eliminated competition from the existing dynamics by channeling it to your own ends. You can then engage the rest of the group as you see fit, because now their whole social structure is both laid open for you as well as reaffirmed for them.

Being in groups of strangers often means losing a frightening degree of control. You can help individuals in an audience feel more secure by offering them a chance to lead. Allowing someone from the group to do your part while you step back and watch them bonds you with the group. You are now part of them, sharing their experience. They have a chance to see and photograph one of their own group in an interesting circumstance. When you can let them lead, you say that they are important, that what they think is important, and that the people they consider important are important to you.

People like to control their own experiences. Interactivity is a way of sharing the power and expressing welcome. Museums have found a wonderful tool called discovery drawers. Where else is it OK to open drawers and see what is in them? At home, in your own house, in a place where you belong. The associations of being free to rummage in drawers are pleasant and privileged. No wonder visitors like it so much. They want to appreciate what they want to appreciate, not what you want them to appreciate. Respect and honor that, and you will build some credit toward yourself and your agenda.

4. Strengthen self-esteem.

Visiting a restored eighteenth-century tavern, I enjoyed the tour given by a charming young lady. I was listening thoughtfully and showing my informed interest by asking revealing and insightful questions. I thought things were going very well and I was relaxing and enjoying the visit. Then we came to the fact that George Washington slept in this tavern on his southern tour. Relaxed and feeling good, I said, "Boy, he slept everywhere! I guess that's why they call him 'The father of our country.'"

Now things had been going pretty well up to this point. But as I laughed, her smile went dead and after a killing pause she said, "You'd be surprised how many times I hear that."

In that instant I felt as if I shrank to the height of a mouse. Any sense of self-worth went skittering under the rug. I remember none

*Show your audience that you think
they are important.*

of the rest of the visit, I remember none of what happened before I
made the comment, but I will never forget what an ass I made of
myself.

Still, who was wrong here? I made an imbecilic joke to fulfill
some pathetic need, but in this context, I was the amateur, and she
was the professional, and unless I was disrupting the group and
this was the only way to correct my behavior, she (the professional)
knocked me out of the picture by pointing up my idiocy. The damage to my self-esteem may have also been apparent to the others in
the group, and they may have raised their guard, no matter how
much they sympathized with our guide. Self-esteem comes before
(but is never a substitute for) the edification you have to offer.

Put someone down and expect them to learn from you? Not
likely. Asking a question of the audience and then saying "wrong!"
embarrasses the person and they will spend the rest of the event
with their attention devoted to defending themselves from you.
Learning is an emotional experience that requires giving up an old
state of knowledge and accepting a new one. You don't need to make
it any harder.

Remember that the audience wants you to succeed. Through their time and physical presence, they have made an investment in you. Positive previsualization works wonders for self-esteem. Get a picture in your mind of how you want to see the audience responding. Enter as winner and see the audience as winners too. Approach the world with trust, respect, and confidence and you will generate more trust, respect, and confidence among others.

Finally, remember the old adage about government, "Never mistake incompetence for malevolence," and extend it to your amateur audience. You, the professional, should make the opening statement of an encounter. If you leave that task to your amateur audience, be prepared then for flippant remarks that many people use to protect themselves from rejection. On the surface, these comments sound hostile and even abusive, but you must translate them to understand them as they are intended. For example:

"You must have really screwed up to have drawn this duty."
actually means
"I find your work very interesting,
I admire your skill already."

and

"Who the hell are you supposed to be?"
actually means
"Excuse me, but would you please share your knowledge of
this place with me?"

If you are a professional communicator, and your audience is composed largely of amateurs, the burden is not equal. Competence in social interactions is a requirement of your job, but not of theirs. Never mistake incompetence for malevolence.

When all of the preceding is tended to, you can promote self-actualization. Only when all the previous needs are met can a person devote attention to fulfilling their potential and benefit from their time with you.

People prefer and are more easily persuaded by people similar to themselves. Mirroring physical behaviors builds rapport with harmonious interaction.

Build Rapport

If there is one thing that all presenters agree on, it's the importance of building trust through the initial contact. "Here is where you reach out to these people," says Marcus Hansen, "you ask questions and they know you're interested in them. There's a kind of a trust that you establish with people. They feel comfortable, they're not intimidated by you in any way—then the highway's open, they can talk to you, you can talk to them, and then you can capitalize like crazy."

Personal rapport with the audience may be based on previous feelings of commonality and goodwill. Prepublicity and a good in-

*Find your initial allies and use them as your base
to build rapport with the rest of the audience.*

troduction can also help. If you are just meeting the audience for the
first time, sharing jokes, mutual concerns, and compliments to the
group bring you closer to them. Sharing anything builds bonds, for
example, participating in a group ritual like passing the peace pipe
before the powwow. Some things are better left unshared, however.
Admitting to nervousness is not productive if you really are nervous. You just might make them nervous too.

People like people similar to themselves, so part of the work of
the introduction is presenting your common ground. Self-deprecating humor works to bring down a perception of superiority, just as
credentials elevate those perceived as inferiors. More fundamentally

though, rapport develops on a visceral, animal channel. Remember, it is not enough to be interested in other people, you must *show* your genuine interest by smiling and laughing when appropriate, looking at them, calling them by their name, making them feel important by listening and talking about their interests, complimenting them. Speak fluently with gestures, eye contact, showing that you are listening and concerned by nodding and "humphing." All of this works when handled naturally and sincerely, but is most disconcerting when exaggerated. I have seen behavior that can only be explained by someone's having read in a book that nodding to show support in meetings was important. You could attach a can of paint to his head and have it well mixed in half a minute.

Keep building rapport by encouraging positive movements. Reward the behaviors that you want to encourage with action. If there are things that you want them to touch, acknowledge and support the touching. Every movement they make toward understanding, toward the new behaviors, must get positive strokes. This doesn't have to be as blatant as throwing candy to contributors (although I have seen this work), but it must be clear. You must give clear feedback throughout. Attentive and responsive behavior makes your audience feel positive and confident. Keep your connection with the audience alive by working from cards, notes, an outline, or from a script that you have written and rewritten often enough that you can do without it, but not from reading a script that keeps you focused on a page. "Your eyes belong to the audience, not to the page."

Use More Immediacy in Your Speech

As your audience builds trust with you they will naturally expect more self-disclosure or personal revelation. If you disclose too little, if you never open up, you may come across as hostile and distant. Worse, though, is sharing too much, too soon—you will come across as maladjusted. Deviations from the expected amount (outside of a comic context) are disturbing and distracting. The appropriate amount is highly contingent and culturally defined. Studies suggest that in Western culture, more self-disclosure is accepted more from women than from men. Upon meeting your audience, start building the trusting, sharing relationship, but don't scare them off by going too far. Your choice of words helps define your closeness. For example, of the two statements below, which sounds more positive, convincing, and honest?

> 1. Some people might think that someone with a voice like yours would have been a good speaker.

> 2. You are a good speaker with an excellent voice.

The difference between the two statements is in their degree of immediacy. Immediacy refers to the "directness and intensity" of verbal communication. The degree of directness and intensity shows how positive you feel about an experience, how convinced you are and honest you are being. Listeners use this factor of your speech to gauge the value and credibility of your presentation. Immediacy engenders feelings of openness and trust, but when the directness and intensity of communication fall below an appropriate level, the listener becomes uninterested or suspicious. Immediacy is easier to talk about when you break it down into the categories devised by psychologists Werner and Mehabrian:

SPATIAL......... The physical distance between yourself and the subject.

TEMPORAL ... How far away you place the subject in time.

PARTIAL .... Referring to a part rather than the whole.

CLASS .... Generalizing about a group, as in "You people . . ."

IMPLICIT ...... Implying the message rather than explicitly stating it.

UNILATERAL. Making it one-sided rather than mutual.

PASSIVE .... Imposed rather than desired. "I had to."

MODIFIED .... Hedging with wimp words.

TEMPORAL   PARTIAL

They *were*   I like *her*
honest men.   organizational
                     ability.

SPATIAL   They *are*   I like   CLASS
              honest   *her.*
Those are the men.   You people
originals.   are so fussy.
     These are the   You are so
     originals.   fussy.

IMMEDIACY

He *failed.*   He did it.

He *was not*   *Perhaps* he
at his best.   did it.
          We respect I agree.
          each other.   MODIFIED
IMPLICIT
                         I *have to*
          They   agree.
          respect
          me.

UNILATERAL   PASSIVE

*Looking at immediacy as the center of a target, the examples of less
immediate statements are farther from the bull's eye, nibbling around
the edges of getting to the point.*

Obviously, you need to say what you mean in the way that you
mean to say it. You express your feelings with more or less directness and intensity as you feel appropriate to the circumstances. Immediacy in verbal communication is one aspect of personal disclo-
sure. As with eye contact and vocal characteristics, you can make
sure your habits are not working against you by objectively evaluating recordings or transcriptions of your work.

Maintain Eye Contact

I can guarantee one thing. Keeping eye contact with your audience will cure more problems than any other strategy. We look at what we are interested in—smiling and looking at your audience shows that you are interested in them. Eye contact also tells you how well you're doing. Not making eye contact is like bowling through a curtain.

That first step is so simple, but all agree that you are lost without it. "It's eye-to-eye contact," says Kristy Spivey. "Every individual, every child in your group deserves to be acknowledged. It's the easiest thing to do, simply by cutting your eyes in their direction. As long as they have been acknowledged, then their self-esteem has been raised—maybe not by much, but it always matters and it has to happen every time."

This kind of courtesy lets folks know you will be playing by the rules: You reduce the perceived risk for them and they can open up.

Eye contact is also the channel they use to speak back to you. Studies show that the amount of eye contact affects perception of competence, intelligence, and self-confidence. Increased eye contact is also a primary tool of persuasiveness. Too much too soon can also be disconcerting. Sustained looking can be taken as hostility or a sexual come-on. All except the boldest liars tend to make less eye contact,

and they tend to overdo it. Making eye contact is almost equal to physically touching someone. It intensifies your impact, strengthening cooperation or resistance depending upon whether you're off to a good or a bad start.

We are particularly tuned in to the subtlest differences in faces. One of the primary anti-counterfeiting measures is making the faces on printed money larger and more detailed. We can immediately tell if something is the slightest bit off . We look for cues around the eyes—pupil dilation, direction of gaze, position of the lower eyelid. Eye contact is one of your best tools, so don't take the advice of cheats who tell you to look just above people's eyes with fake contact. It tells you nothing and marks you as a fraud.

Eyes reveal subtleties, as well as the most blatant messages. It's easy to detect when people's eyes glaze over or their attention wanders. You can't always tell if people have learned all your informational goals, but you can usually tell whether they are interested or intrigued. Remember that if you do succeed in stimulating a new

thought, people may need time to integrate it. If they move their eyes off from you to process new information, you have not lost them, you have reached them.

Although you (the professional in this game) have to be totally tuned in to receiving the signals of your audience, you must be equally adept in con-

trolling your own transmissions. On days when you don't feel good, you can't let it show. When you're answering that same question for the thousandth time, you have to be able to answer as if it is the first time.

Your audience is made up of individuals, and an appeal may not work for the entire audience, but if you can win over a significant part of the audience, the rest will probably follow. Speak directly to one pair of sympathetic eyes after another until you have made contact all about the room. People in the center and front of the audience may be the most favorably disposed to you; that's why they sat front and center. Start with them and work outward. People on the edges may have reasons for standing where they can make a graceful exit. Don't worry if they drift away. They're holding back to begin with and by concentrating on them you could be pulled away from your core audience.

Individuals check visually with the others around them, particularly the more influential members of the group, to see if their response is similar. If they see that the others are interested, they will have to ask themselves why they are not. Stacking the deck on this behavior is an old technique. Leni Riefenstahl's propaganda film *Triumph of the Will* is rife with shots of "ordinary Germans" nodding in awed approval of the Nazi party line. This need for confirmation from others in the group is why we have laugh tracks and audience reaction shots in mass media.

So find your allies in the audience and use them to build your strength. Comedian Steve Martin once spoke about how his early material was challenging to his audiences, but he still believed in it and played to the waiters at the comedy clubs who began catching on after a few nights of seeing his act. They became "insiders" and their laughter and understanding helped the rest of the audience become insiders. Pretty soon, he said, "I was playing to an entire audience of insiders, and that's what you want."

All of this is building to the transformative moment when the audience accepts you as their guide, their mentor. Your behavior will have an impact beyond the expansion of the audience's knowledge. They will trust your modeling of appropriate relationships to the environment and others. Demonstrating your trust in yourself as well as your trust in them shows that they have brought their brains to the right place. They are not going to discover merely how brilliant and insightful you are; it's much better. They are about to discover how brilliant and insightful *they* are.

CHAPTER 5
HOLD THEIR INTEREST

Interest is the catalyst that drives the mind to unite ideas and establish relationships. Thinking is work, work that is sparked only by the pleasurable feelings of interest. It is as bad to foolishly ignore the elements that interest your audience as it is to knavishly bury your content in superfluous razzle-dazzle. As one preacher put it, "Dullness is a sin, because it stands between your congregation and the word of God." A sinfully dull presentation may be deadly, but unless we hold it synonymous with sloth, it is not among the seven deadly sins. For that matter, tales of pride, envy, gluttony, lust, anger, and covetousness can be mighty interesting. But these are only subsets of the seven fundamental factors of interest. They are:

SIGNIFICANCE .... Audience connections with your content.

UNIQUENESS .... "You'll never see another one like this!"

HUMOR .... The delight of the unexpected.

PROBLEMS .... Active engagement in finding solutions.

CONCRETENESS .... Illustrating the abstract with the tangible.

ANTAGONISM .... Struggling to overcome opposition.

VARIATION.............. Repeating the idea in different forms.

Given a choice, people will seek out their own interests and pursue them most diligently. All you have to do is stock the shelves and get out of the way. If, however, you want to direct interest into a new area, exploiting these seven factors will draw people in. We'll look at each of these factors in turn.

Significance

Exhausted from museum crawling, I seized a spot on a bench in the gems and minerals exhibit at the Smithsonian. The place was packed with a lava flow of visitors oozing down the corridor. The people shuffled by, knowing that at the end of the path was the fabulous Hope diamond. The stones before me were unremarkable, and most glanced over them expressionless. Every so often, though, someone would perk up at the greenish rocks and say, "Oh! alexandrite!" or "Look Jenny, it's alexandrite!" I had just begun the transition from noticing this phenomenon to wondering about its cause when one person said "Oh look, alexandrite! That's my birthstone!" And, true enough, about every twelfth person perked up and took notice of the rock, because of its personal significance to them.

This is significance. Your name, your hobby, your future, your interests, your past, your you! Where would you fit in? How would you respond? Would you be brave enough? We look for ourselves in every story. Significance through birthstones seems mighty superficial beside the realm of science and knowledge, yet it was the hook that drew in individuals to learn more about "their" alexandrite. Personal significance gets an emotional foot in the door.

One of the easiest ways to interest people is to be interested in them and to find things that they are already interested in. Study your audience. Put yourself in their place and try to see the experience from their viewpoint. Step out of the center of the universe and visualize yourself as being in the audience so you can decide what to do, what not to do, what to put in, what to leave out. Ask yourself, "What would be the best experience if I could think like the audience?" and then work to create that.

Choose an interesting subject for the audience at hand.

Just because you find a topic significant does not necessarily mean that your audience will. Nothing is more boring than other people's children. From the commercial point of view, many industrial presentations are mandated to tell audiences the story of the company's founding egos. Who cares? Not the audience.

Sometimes the urge to "set people straight" becomes overwhelming. You can believe that the information you have is so right and so important that it must be conveyed at all costs. But if your audience is interested in something else, you have to be willing to work with them, and not say, "Well, that's not the important thing, the important thing is that . . ." Then you're not talking with your people, you're just talking to yourself.

If the subject is interesting—to the audience—you are way ahead in the game. Individuals within groups may have a wide diversity of interests, but with any audience, they are interested in themselves.

Show your interest in them and their relationship to the subject. If you are in an interactive, small-group presentation, you have the opportunity to find out the areas of significance by asking questions. One of the tiredest appeals is to geographic affiliations. This ingratiating technique ranges from "Any New Yorkers in the audience tonight? Well, give yourself a big hand!" to "Ich bin ein Berliner!"

Mass media searches for the largest possible audience by resorting to the lowest common denominator, generally, the problems associated with dominance and mating. Still, even the most difficult work panders to the interests of the audience, small though it may be. What subject do you think would interest an audience of paint-drying technologists? Obviously it will be easier to interest a convention of bridge builders in an advanced lecture on bridges than it will be to interest a general audience, until you build or reveal bridges of significance to them. Put the audience in the picture. Show the audience the famous film of the bridge "Galloping Gertie" as it whips, twists, and finally collapses. "Imagine yourself in the middle of this span high over the Tacoma Narrows. Now, as you plummet toward the water along with the wreckage of the bridge, you might wonder, 'How did this happen to me?'"

Another way to engage through significance is with sympathetic characters. How many times have you heard a reviewer pan a movie because "we don't care about the characters." We don't care because we find no significant correlation to our own experience, our own bank of stories. Convincing and engaging stories are full of character details that correlate to stories we already know. Think of this as striking a bell near another bell that shares some of the same tones; the second bell will start to resonate in sympathetic vibration.

Political leaders often try to create a personal story with which many people can identify. Messianic religious leaders even try to get people to adopt the stories they tell as their own. "His/her story is my story." In Robert Penn Warren's great tale of the education of a demagogue, *All the King's Men*, the character Willie Stark learns how to grab his audience with appeals to personal significance.

"I have a speech here," he said. "It is a speech about what this state needs. But there's no use telling you what this state needs. You are the state. You know what you need. Look at your pants. Have they got holes in the knee? Listen to your belly. Did it ever rumble for emptiness? Look at your crop. Did it ever rot in the field because the road was so bad you couldn't get it to market? Look at your kids. Are they growing up ignorant as you and dirt because there isn't any school for them?"

Willie paused, and blinked around the crowd. "No," he said, "I'm not going to read you any speech. You know what you need better'n I could tell you. I'm going to tell you a story."

Willie Stark is a good guy at this point, but his growing power inevitably corrupts him. Appeals to significance, as with all of these techniques, are a neutral tool, used equally for good and evil. Mastery of these techniques simply gives you power.

One powerful technique Willie Stark employs in this example is frequent use of the word "you." Saying "you" puts the audience in the story. At a seminar on the history of slavery, our presenter used this technique to place us in the position of both the slave and the slave-merchant in turn. She said, "*You* are packed in the ship, chained head to foot. *You* first have to survive the passage," followed by advice to the slave-ship owner: "*You* don't want to pack together people from the same language group—*you* might have a problem." Our changing imaginary roles were clearly defined, and infinitely more engaging than the distant, amorphous "*They would have been chained together . . .*"

Using personal names, small-group exercises, participation, individual feedback—all put the individuals in the picture so the event is partially about them. Interest through significance declines as we move away from ourselves. First we like to hear about ourselves, then about people like ourselves, then our families, our tribes, our nation, our species. What if your subject is not human? Like dogs and other dogs, people are interested in other people. Oversolicitous presenters will try to put everything in human terms for us. On a nature trail I encountered a sign interpreting the thorny catbrier vine as "Aptly called 'nature's barbed wire'." Now the catbrier vine may resemble barbed wire, but we can assume that nature did not copy the human product. Anthropomorphism and other techniques to help the audience "relate" to the subject can easily foster silliness and inaccuracy.

Significance puts the audience members into the center of the universe. But this narcissistic "what's in it for me?" factor is easily overindulged. If your content is too personalized, too customized to existing interests, what happens to growth? You risk treating your audience like babies that are only interested in confirming themselves.

But you knew that.

Uniqueness

Back at the Smithsonian gems and minerals exhibit, all humans were flowing to one point, toward the one rock that they know by name and legend. All of the other gems were only warm-up acts for the one, the only, the fabled Hope diamond. Of course the Hope diamond doesn't send out magnetic uniqueness rays that pull people toward it. Rather, we have interested ourselves with an elaborate construction of stories that, added to the diamond's striking physical attributes, makes this particular carbon ball unique. Through agreement, we have defined this rock as a goal, much as we would identify a particular tree as "base" in a game of tag. As an element of interest, it is the perception of, rather than the fact of, uniqueness that draws us in. The Hope diamond is truly singular, truly unique, but in fact, so are you and every person you meet.

People are forced into conformity, but when we are allowed to perceive their uniqueness, when they confound our expectations of them, they become more interesting. Nonconformists, from Marx to the Marx Brothers, stand out in our minds when they present un-common, undesirable, or unexpected behaviors. People known for extraordinary goodness, wickedness, skill, or bravery are blatantly unique. Knowing this, you might trot out all the oddities around your subject, upstaging other elements of interest. Uniqueness thus overdone becomes a drawback. Indulgence in the bizarre can obscure a subject as readily as rendering it commonplace in an effort to help your audience relate to it.

From an individual's perspective, novelty is a degree of uniqueness, and novelty can be threatening. Something that is so strange and new that it cannot be associated with any past experience can be tough for your audience to get their brains around and they may reject it. Your audience may need something to hang on to. They may reject a novel approach to a novel subject, but a familiar approach to a novel subject or a novel approach to a familiar subject gives their brains a place to stand while they work on the idea.

Something commonplace to one person may be unique (and interesting) to another. It may be a unique context for commonplace things that becomes interesting. I don't suspect too many travelers have been drawn off the road by billboards touting "SEE FOUR-LEGGED PIG!" But we might walk well out of our way to see that same pig loose on Broadway. A dollar bill found tucked under your windshield wiper is not interesting because you have never seen a dollar bill before, but because you discovered it in a place where you usually find bad news.

Even the unique can become commonplace if presented in a commonplace manner. The "old hat" presentation sometimes needs a creative new hat. Imagine an approach to your subject from an unfamiliar point of view. How might the factory look today to one of its first workers? What would a servant's-eye view of the great house be like?

Your need to create new approaches never ends. Innovation begets imitation, and what was singular becomes commonplace far sooner than we think. You can strengthen your position by engaging innovation on the micro level as well as by changing the big picture. Draw upon your imagination to see the experience from every audience's perspective and keep finding ways to let them become co-creators, free to exploit the potentially unique aspects of their moments with you.

Uniqueness does not have to be the world's only geothermally powered bicycle. Uniqueness is also the product of your creative efforts to bring experiences into the moment. Live presentations will always give more of a sense of singularity than recorded ones. Activities that allow more participation, that respond to the presence of the audience and the unique circumstances of the environment, will be more interesting. There is only one you—your individuality, your honest expression of self is found nowhere else. Your audience and you have never been together before in precisely this circumstance. Your hearty embrace of your specific time, story, audience, and self will always be uniquely interesting.

Humor

This house, once owned by Noah Webster, was sold for a time to Yale University, where it served as a fraternity house.
(pause)
But, as you can see, it is still standing.

guide at Greenfield Village museum

Do you like to laugh? Well, so does your audience: Humor is reported as the number one "liked" characteristic of presenters. Humor engages our thoughts and feelings; even to laugh at someone slipping on a banana peel you must have an attitude toward the person who slips. You must perceive the tension of a person's superiority before it can be relieved by undignified downfall. When the tension is resolved through a new and unexpected path in your brain, the feeling is called humorous. Humor is a guilty pleasure—a slightly naughty trick of the mind both reprimanded and rewarded by laughter. Look at all the good that humor does:

- Humor gives permission for creative activity and encourages divergent thinking.
- The brain represents only 2 percent of your body weight, yet it consumes a quarter of your oxygen intake. Laughing out loud oxygenates your blood and feeds the brain.
- All humor can be used to entertain, to keep the audience interested, but related to the subject at hand, humor can be used to further your point.
- Humor, as a "high-contrast" event, provides an emotionally embedding hook for memory.
- Laughter gives a unit of success, a moment of "getting it," to reward paying attention within a larger body of material, where the reward is less immediate.
- Jokes are self-replicating, subversive memes. They are told and retold, spreading like an infectious germ.

> • Laughing together is a shared experience that bonds the group.

Self-deprecating humor helps to diminish the distance between you and the audience. As mentioned earlier, Ron Popeil (inventor of the Veg-O-Matic) began his career selling kitchen gadgets to passersby at state fairs. Singing his words like a carnival barker, holding on to the last syllable of every sentence so there is no chance to escape, he drew people in with his humor. With the Veg-O-Matic he would busily slice away while proclaiming "You can cut an onion so thin it has only one side!" "You can cut a tomato so thin it will last all winter!" With these preposterous claims he attracted attention, developed positive orientation toward himself, and disarmed the feelings of skepticism that we have learned to apply to salesmen.

Feeling that you are a part of a group is a basic human need, and groups are bonded by laughter. In the radio series *A Prairie Home Companion*, Garrison Keillor alternately celebrates and ridicules the values of the audience. His vehicle is a comedic variant on Protestant church services with the regular singing, character lessons, and closing sermon. Those who tune in each week get the secret jokes, meanings that bring you within the congregation, within the family.

The essence of humor is sharing and enjoying one another. All compact humor is based on a setup to get us going in one direction and a punch line to dump us off at an unexpected destination. From this new viewpoint we look back along the path of the surprise connection and "get" the joke. The setup and the punch must contrast. The setups must be brief, honest, and realistic, followed by escalating punch lines. Using the joke-mapping strategy developed by creativity authority Edward de Bono, we see how the common forms follow this same pattern.

Each joke follows the cycle of the setup, the creation of expectations in the real world, followed by the "sharp left turn" of the punch line, then the audience's laughter as they make the connection, while they, depending upon the convention of the presentation, see your continued emotional relationship to the material and/or your appreciation for their response, followed by the next line just after the laughter peaks.

The joke is the atomic unit of minds on communication. It begins where the audience is and takes them along with you. For your audience to get a joke, you have your work to do and they have theirs. First, you have to set it up well, let them work on it, then deliver the punch line at just the right moment; then they have to make the connections to "get" it. A good training class uses the same structure of tension and resolution. So does a good mystery, drama, or sales pitch.

Humor follows this tension–unexpected resolution structure because of the way we think. Listening is a process of guessing ahead for meaning. The realistic setup leads your audience along one path, which experience tells them should have an expected logical out-

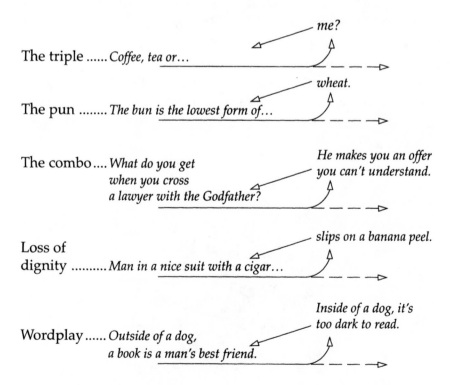

The triple ...... *Coffee, tea or...* *me?*

The pun .... *The bun is the lowest form of...* *wheat.*

The combo .... *What do you get when you cross a lawyer with the Godfather?* *He makes you an offer you can't understand.*

Loss of dignity .... *Man in a nice suit with a cigar...* *slips on a banana peel.*

Wordplay ...... *Outside of a dog, a book is a man's best friend.* *Inside of a dog, it's too dark to read.*

come, but they are forced to jump to an entirely different destination with the punch line. When they have fallen through a hole in their neural net and landed in another one, the result is humor. They see a connection, but it is not the one they expected.

Henri Bergson observed that we laugh when we see people acting inflexibly like a machine. We also laugh when we see a person act like an animal, or a machine act like a human. As I wrote this my dog walked through some weeds and came out with a flowering vine around his neck. I laughed at the happy accident that made my dog seem to act with human vanity.

Beyond telling jokes, the deeper level of humor is the revelation of personal pain and struggle. This reveals (but doesn't unload) your fears, loves, status, weaknesses, pomposity, appearance—all reflected in a fun house mirror. This humor reveals your personal attitude to a subject, even if that subject is yourself. When asked how he felt about his party's loss of the New York elections, Abraham Lincoln responded, "I feel somewhat like the boy in Kentucky who stubbed his toe while running to see his sweetheart. The boy said he was too big to cry but far too badly hurt to laugh."

Deep humor requires that you own the emotional connection to the material. This is why you easily bomb using someone else's material. You can generate your own material by shaping your ex-

perience into the recognizable humorous forms. No matter what your life experience has given you, there is plenty that can be mined, refined, and forged into the structures of humor, such as those mapped out earlier, as well as the forms below:

callbacks .... A running gag, a reference back to an earlier gag.
compare/contrast "You know the difference between . . ."
exaggeration .... "It's so dry I saw two trees fighting over a dog."
incongruity .... A luxury car being towed by a team of oxen.
irony .... "The fireplace channel, all hardwood—all the time."
list making .... "Let's see, you've got your . . ."
mimicry .... "I love the tone of voice they use when . . ."
observations .... "Did you ever notice how . . ."
parody .... Uses familiar works as the vehicle for satire.
sarcasm .... "Hey. Nice paint job!"
satire .... Exaggerates and exposes the follies of society.
shtick .... A repeated characteristic that confirms expectations.
slapstick .... Low physical comedy based on the loss of dignity.
switcheroo .... Logical inversion. "I love getting audited, because now they have to . . ."
unexpected .... You open a piano lid and find a sleeping cat.
wit .... "It is characteristic of wit to penetrate into the hidden depths of things, to pick out some telling circumstance or relation, by noting which the whole object appears in a new and clearer light." —*George Santayana*

Using your background and these formats, you can create new material based on yourself, common experience with the audience, and the subject at hand. Don't, however, inflict untested new material on a real audience; that's what friends and family are for. Children of professional comedians have told me that they never considered their parent very funny, probably because their mom or dad was trying out all their new ideas on them. The dud material was tried and died at home; only the winners went public.

Even the most spontaneous-appearing performers, such as Robin Williams, carefully structure and rehearse their material. Your initial material must establish the common ground, the bond with your audience you will build upon throughout the presentation. Start where they are and take them along with you. Once you establish the connection and begin developing intimacy you can venture into more daring territory. Should you begin to disconnect from the audience, however, if you're losing them, don't speed up and try to rush through to the end. Rather, slow down and rebuild the connection. A bad thing done faster is just over sooner—it's still not good.

The amount and kind of humor you use in a presentation depend upon the circumstances. If you are doing pure entertainment, you must deliver a punch line at a rate varying from every ten seconds to every three minutes. Of course, many circumstances simply do not require a display of your wit. Take care to give the audience some warning if you are about to change gears. Throwing in a joke at the end of a serious presentation ignores the whole process of building closeness to the audience. It can fall as flat as the guide on the jungle cruise ride who ends the robotic gag-fest with "But seriously, folks, we do need to save the rain forests."

Many people are afraid of humor because it might hurt their message, but humor has no impact on credibility, only on increasing likability. This does not mean that humor cannot be used inappropriately. It shouldn't take up all the time if the audience is hoping for more information. Run a cost/benefit analysis on your humor factor. Abraham Lincoln was regularly accused of making humorous commentary on inappropriate occasions. Consider the effect of your humor on your other agreements with your audience. If your work has a chronological convention to it (you're speaking from a historical time perspective), don't violate it for the sake of a joke. Also, there are limited arenas where stories about Pilgrims cohabiting with barnyard animals are helpful. The ghost of Santayana looms, warning that "fun is a good thing, but only when it spoils nothing better."

Problems

Give your audience work to do. As Laurent Daloz writes, "The trip belongs, after all, to the traveler, not the guide." Asking your audience to solve problems with you plays right into a basic human need to reduce our level of uncertainty. When a gap develops between our thoughts and our actions, we work to close it. Asking the audience to bridge a gap with you is an expression of trust as you turn over more control of the experience to them. You enter into a partnership with them, like a skillful rider who knows when to let the horse do some of the work of finding the path. You are choosing the destination, but you and the horse have to get there together.

Sometimes you don't know what kind of horse you have. Informal encounters with varied audiences can leave you without clues as to the educational background of individuals. The person in the tank top and goofy hat might well be far better informed than you—they are just dressed stupidly. They are with you to benefit from your specialized knowledge, not to admire a display of your imagined superiority.

If you question the audience, they can infer that they have the right to question you back. Whenever possible, encourage this by responding to questions when they come up rather than making your audience hold them until the end. The questions people ask are valuable feedback to help show you what level of challenge is most appropriate.

Reward curiosity, don't punish it. You are the professional, so cut some slack for your amateur questioners. Every question calls for a respectful response. Keep your audience in the game by asking for help when the question is unclear. Just say, "I need you to help me with that, to make sure I understand your question. Are you asking if . . . ?" The audience will trust you if you work quickly and successfully to find the right level of challenge. If you pose a problem to an audience, be prepared to quickly offer a series of hints that make the solution progressively easier. Seek the right level from the top down, checking for comprehension as you go. The audience should have most of the puzzle pieces before you ask them to put them together.

The audience needs good work to do. Not opening gaps for them to bridge, making the gaps too small, or bridging them for the audience implies that they are incapable of growth. They will become bored and resent your condescending attitude. But what if a problem is too tough? Then the dissonance is with their self-image. When a problem is posed, they think they should be able to solve it because they are as smart as the next guy. Success closes the gap by confirming their self-image. Failure requires another bridging method. When the fox can't get the grapes, he creates the fiction that the grapes were sour. If you pose problems that keep the grapes always out of reach for everyone but you, how will your audience close the gap?

Some of the problems you can pose for an audience require no answer. They are simple sensory tasks where you ask them to listen, touch, smell, taste, look. "Can you smell the bread baking from here?" "Can you feel the machinery shaking the building right now?" Don't disparage physical problems. There is a German proverb, "Griffen bedeutet begriffen," meaning "Grasping with the hands means grasping with the mind." Hands-on problems allow for the acquisition of nonverbal knowledge. They also get another part of the mind

But all I did was to tell them what I was going to tell 'em, tell 'em, tell 'em what I told 'em, tell 'em what I was going to tell 'em I told 'em, when I was telling 'em what...

engaged, giving the more calculating, rational part of the mind a chance to get some rest. Even the simplest problems generate interest. "See if you can get this apart, put this together, help me move this, look in that cupboard for it, tell me if you like this."

One method of generating a variety of questions appears on the following pages. I took seven cognitive tasks (plus simple sensory awareness), combined them with Gardner's eight intelligences, and arranged the two octets on a pair of flattened-out dice. Constructing and rolling the dice will give you sixty-four possible combinations of problems for your audience to work on.

Sharing problems should not become repetitive in form or draw attention to itself. Questions, role-playing, raising hands, letting the audience generate the agenda, discussions, brainstorming, debates, written activities, case studies, contests, games, physical activities, skill practices, panel discussions, and break-out groups—all can involve problem solving.

Problem solving works in sales too. Like all good salesmen, Ron Popeil used demonstrations of a problem to interest his audience, to turn passersby into customers. He would set up the problem—the grape juice stain on the rug, the dangerous slicer—showing the inadequacies of the old way. "But wait! So you think this carpet is ruined! Now let's try . . ." He could then show the advantage of his product, having interested the audience in solving a problem that presented itself right before their eyes. Engaging you with setup problems and then offering a product as the solution is a most ancient advertising form.

Problem solving works on the macro level of the experience as well. If people have an individual hypothesis to test, they will be more interested in the whole experience. They may bring this personal agenda with them, or you can offer one. Upon entering the Holocaust Museum in Washington, D.C., you receive a card identifying an actual individual who may or may not have survived the war. At the end of the visit, after learning about the events and how different groups were affected, you place your card in a machine that tells you the fate of your individual. My card was a Polish man, a high school mechanics teacher. I followed the events depicted through the museum, wondering what might happen to him as if he were someone I knew. At the end of my visit, I placed his card in the machine, expecting the worst—and the worst is what I found.

Like most powerful messages, this idea of following an individual through the Holocaust grabs you through many of the elements of interest. It appeals to significance through your identification with the individual; it is a unique approach causing you to work on the problem of whether they survive; you have a concrete, specific individual to follow through the abstract mayhem of the time; antagonism between sweeping events and your individual's fate pervades your experience; and your individual varies from those acquired by the others in your group. In this case, however, there was no attempt to appeal to humor.

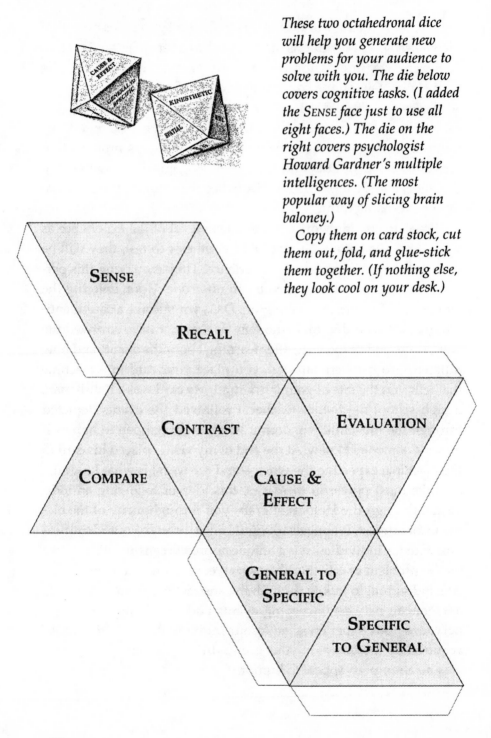

These two octahedronal dice will help you generate new problems for your audience to solve with you. The die below covers cognitive tasks. (I added the SENSE face just to use all eight faces.) The die on the right covers psychologist Howard Gardner's multiple intelligences. (The most popular way of slicing brain baloney.)

Copy them on card stock, cut them out, fold, and glue-stick them together. (If nothing else, they look cool on your desk.)

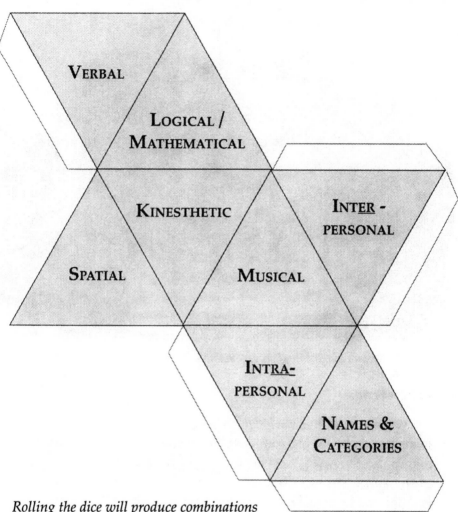

Rolling the dice will produce combinations such as CAUSE & EFFECT with KINESTHETIC shown on the previous page. An example of a problem using this combination in a discovery setting might be the classic hold-a-spinning-bicycle-wheel-while-sitting-on-a-swivel-stool demonstration of gyroscopic stabilization. Having experienced the effect of the gyroscope, then ask the audience to simulate the effects of gyro-stabilization if it were applied to automobiles.

The Foucault pendulum gives a concrete demonstration of earth's rotation.

Concreteness

William Strunk in his *Elements of Style* wrote that "the surest way to arouse and hold the attention of the reader is by being specific, definite and concrete." At the hearings investigating the explosion of the space shuttle Challenger, physicist Richard Feynman cut through the technical mumbo-jumbo with a simple demonstration. Sitting at his desk before the commission, he replicated the failure of the rubber O-rings by placing a compressed sample in a glass of ice water and showed how it failed to return to its original shape. Although this was, as communications authority Edward R. Tufte described it, just a "colorful theater of physics" rather than a controlled experiment, it achieved Feynman's goal. It made the point that could have prevented the disaster to begin with—low temperatures make gaskets fail and rockets explode.

Educator Larry Earl has some of the best technique I have ever seen in making a notoriously boring experience concrete and exciting. Given the task of presenting a tour of a historic house (and this could work just as well or better in a nuclear power plant), rather than the usual "Please-feel-free-to-look-in-any-of-the-rooms-and-if-you-have-any-questions-I'll-be-happy-to-answer-them" approach, Larry gives the house tour a touch of mischief. Larry begins your visit by establishing himself as the butler Benjamin, a role he will step in and out of seamlessly throughout the visit. First he tells you about how he is sizing you up as to whether he will admit you into the house or not. But since you appear to be the right kind of people he escorts you into the parlor. Because the master of the house is away at present, he says that Ben is going to ask you to wait in the parlor while he goes to bring some refreshments from the kitchen.

Now considering that Ben is a slave, and really doesn't have too much hope for advancement, Larry asks you if Ben is likely to hurry or take his own sweet time. You agree that he is more likely to take his own sweet time. Larry now says, "Let's think about it. Ben has got to walk all the way back to the kitchen, that's one minute. He's going to talk to Julia the cook for a little bit. That's two minutes. He's going to get himself something to eat, that's another two minutes. Then he's got to walk all the way back here, that's another minute. That's a total of six minutes that you are left alone in somebody's house. Now what do you do when you are left alone in somebody's house?" "Snoop around!" comes a voice from the crowd. "Oh, you know!" says Larry, not missing a beat. "So you got time now to look upstairs and down. We'll meet back here in six minutes and act like nothing happened. Don't get caught!"

Assuming that his portrait of Ben is historically responsible, Larry has accomplished several strong tasks. One of the historical members of the household has been brought to life by concrete, quantitative, chronological narrative of a slice of his life. The enhanced awareness created by tension of the playful mischief of "snooping around" makes the visitors notice more, think faster, and remember better as ownership of the experience is pushed to them. (Another staff member is normally stationed upstairs so security is not an issue.) Remember, this was Larry's choice, his determination of how to make the tour interesting. He could have done the generic "Old-house, old-chairs, take-a-look-up-the-stairs" tour. Instead, he gave of his creative self, showing respect for his audience as well as his subject.

Concrete expressions generate power through specific images that we can see, hear, touch, taste, smell. Ahab's nemesis was not just a whale, not just a great white whale, it was a great white whale with a proper name. When Martin Luther King, Jr., gave his "I have a dream" speech on the steps of the Lincoln Memorial, he used a concrete image for the unfulfilled promise of racial equality. He spoke of a "check written to the American negro" that had been returned for "insufficient funds." This concrete metaphor for general injustice made clear the sense of a broken legal and moral obligation.

Large numbers are also notoriously hard to grasp. This has generated the ubiquitous concrete equivalency metaphor—"That's enough energy to power nine supertankers nine times around the world." Like all effective techniques, it has long been overused. When this happens, you can sideslip one technique into another, just as Dorothy Parker did when she observed that "if all the girls in attendance at the Yale Prom were laid end to end, I wouldn't be the least bit surprised."

Inevitably, our drive to shape amorphous phenomena into concrete categories causes distortion. One of our consultants returned from a conference with a catchphrase stating that individuals had degrees of interest in exhibits corresponding to the categories of "streakers, strollers, and scholars." Others picked this up and repeated it at meetings and in reports. It reduced the complex palette of behaviors to three primary colors. To some, it implied taking a triage approach to audiences—paying attention only to the "strollers." In the intellectual equivalent of Gresham's law, this overly simple analogy drove the more nuanced descriptions of audience behavior out of circulation. But as a catchphrase, it was unstoppable. "Streakers, strollers, and scholars" had alliteration, it was a triad, and the naughtiness of the word "streakers" gave it spice. Simpler, more concrete packages are easier to understand, and are usually better accepted than more complex interpretations of reality.

Antagonism

We try to deny it, but everyone loves a good fight. Whether it be human against human, against nature, against fate, or against self, struggle is interesting. After watching Hamlet struggle with his indecision and a few good sword fights, Londoners could leave the Globe theater and walk a short distance to watch bears and dogs forced to tear each other apart. Today we can enjoy the same violence applied to political debate on our televisions. From "Nature red in tooth and claw" to "If it bleeds, it leads," antagonism has long been the lowest common denominator of interest.

It is easy to speculate about an evolutionary reason for our interest in antagonism. Social beings need to see who the winners and losers are within the group. By watching, we also learn how to compete better when it comes our turn to fight. The compelling attraction of antagonism has been ritualized into sports and dramas. It is the essential ingredient of life on the small screen.

Antagonism is just as prone to becoming a distraction as the other elements of interest. Dale Carnegie wrote that "the best argument is that which seems merely an explanation." Now it seems the reverse is true. Linguist Deborah Tannen, in her book *The Argument Culture,* pointed out the reflexive drive to exploit antagonism in the mass media. If an expert on the persecution of the Jews by the Nazis is invited to speak on a television program, the producers, in order to make the program more "interesting," may also invite someone who denies that the Holocaust ever happened. For the sake of argument, but donning the mask of "balance," they willingly sacrifice the advance of knowledge and legitimize pathological mendacity.

Such abuse aside, antagonism is essential where it is expected. Drama is conflict. A drama is interesting to the extent that a protagonist struggles to overcome obstacles in order to achieve a goal. If there is a dramatic story at the heart of your message, find it and use it. Who remembers Apollo 12 and 14? It is the life-and-death struggle of the Apollo 13 astronauts that holds our interest. The pioneers in a field hold more interest for us than those who came later, as their story will be filled with struggle. A story without struggle is simply not dramatic, and if you have led the audience to expect drama, leaving out the struggle leaves them bored.

Antagonism also works well in lower doses. Struggling with a task is often more interesting than when everything runs smoothly. Antagonism is also the action that reveals the truth of your story. Showing the failures—the throwaways when casting an engine block—reveals reality. Watching someone get the buttons out of sequence on their shirt reveals how nervous they are about an upcoming event. As Garrison Keillor's fictional radio program manager said, "The more mistakes the better! Goofs were better than anything we could plan." Sometimes that true.

The Bear Gardne

The Globe

Variation

Lack of productive variation is the chief cause of boring presentations. As the lady said upon hearing of a friend who was in labor for thirty-six hours, "Listen, I don't even want to do something that feels *good* for thirty-six hours."

Variation is too often an element of interest because it comes as such a relief, but it is most effective when it also supports the other attributes of your presentation. Quicker cutting with shorter scenes is a standard cinematic technique to reinforce the building excitement as a story approaches the climax. Within a narrative presentation, increasing rate and volume should support the rising action of the plot.

Isolating variables such as rate of speech can reveal their effectiveness in contributing to the dramatic effect. I videotaped two presenters telling the story of the Wright brothers' first flight. Below, the two presentations are distilled to show only the rate of speech in words-per-minute measured at 30-second intervals. Looking just at these two plots, which of the two presentations do you think lost 50 percent of its audience due to walkouts?

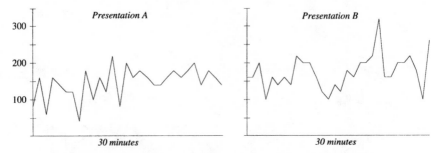

Variation in rate of speech plotted in words per minute.

As you probably chose correctly, 23 of the 45 audience members walked out before the conclusion of presentation A. Presentation B lost only 5 of the 51 people in its audience.

The significant difference is the way the two presenters used variation in rate of speech to reinforce the narrative. Both presentations told the story of the Wright brothers, beginning with their childhood, chronicling their struggles up to their climatic first flight in 1903, followed by their quest for recognition and patent protection. Whereas presentation A rambles on with little organized change in rate of speech, presentation B strongly mirrors and emphasizes the dramatic structure of the plot. The peak in presentation B comes precisely at the moment of the successful flight. The vocally boring presentation (A) also shows a slower average rate of speech. It is a picture of plodding monotony, and failure to interest as the minds (and in this case, the bodies) of the audience wander off in search of engagement.

Posture and gesture also reinforce the ideas and feelings contained in communication, including our attitude toward the audience. Open, varied, and free expressions imply liking and social closeness. We can isolate this variation as well. These two series of samples

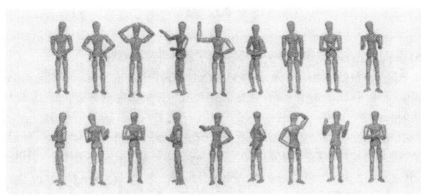

from a training film for tour guides show the varied postures of an instructor demonstrating the "good" and "bad" ways to reach an audience. These samples were taken at ten-second intervals throughout the two three-minute videotaped presentations. Based solely on the "body language," which of the two presentations do you find more interesting?

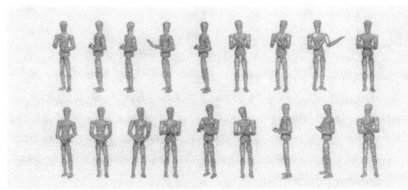

Most viewers agree that the more open and expressive postures in the first series are more interesting than the closed and excessively formal postures of the second series. The clincher is, the first, more interesting series actually shows the instructor's demonstration of "bad" technique. The visually boring series is the "good" way to do the job. Such training is "not only dull in itself, it is the cause of dullness in others." In truth, the verbal content of the "bad" presentation was dithering and unfocused, even though the physical content is clear, honest, and engaging. The second series was far more verbally coherent and informative (if you read the transcript)

but the unnaturally constrained posture, narrow vocal range, and fixed smile detract from its superior intellectual content and alienate the audience from the messenger and the message.

Meaningful variation in the tonal qualities of your voice also helps you to transmit your intelligence. First, look at a sample from Ben Stein's classic portrayal of the boring teacher in *Ferris Bueller's Day Off*. This spectrogram and the ones that follow show the tonal variation within 7.5-second-long samples of recorded speech. Time moves from left to right, and the vertical scale shows the pitch of the voice from 100 Hz (G two octaves below middle C) at the bottom and 1500 Hz (G two octaves above middle C) at the top. The darkness of a band shows its power. The multiple bands show the resonance and overtones of the voice, the microphone, and the room.

Ben Stein as the "Teacher"

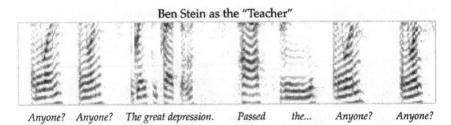

Anyone?   Anyone?   The great depression.   Passed   the...   Anyone?   Anyone?

The elevated, closely packed bands of Ben Stein's character show his high-frequency, nasal head resonance. He varies his tone upward on "Anyone?" to communicate a question, but he precisely repeats this expression at measured intervals. It is the archetypal interpretation of a boring performance.

Boring Tour Guide

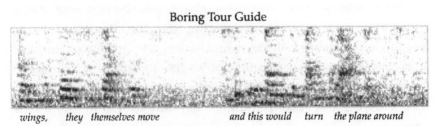

wings,   they   themselves move   and this would   turn   the plane around

A truly boring presentation has much less to offer. Above is the speaker on the Wright brothers who had most of his audience walk out. The individual words are flat and unmodulated—all in the same tonal range. The grey "snow" running all the way across the bottom of the spectrogram is the sound of the air conditioning in the room. His voice barely has the energy to show through the background.

Rev. Dr. Martin Luther King, Jr.'s "Promised Land" speech

about anything! I'm not   fearing   any man!   Mine   eyes   have seen the glory of the coming of the Lord!

Look now at a sample from one of the greatest speakers of the twentieth century—the Rev. Dr. Martin Luther King, Jr., making his "Promised Land" speech. His chest resonance fills the room and the expressive dynamics and power of his voice even punch through the applause and cheering of his audience at the end of this sample.

You can also introduce variation into a presentation by adding multiple characters. When these characters have divergent viewpoints you also have the element of conflict, and appeal to significance by giving the audience someone to identify with as their champion. Conflict can also raise the energy level and the rate of speech so that there is less opportunity for minds to wander off.

Cokie Roberts   William Kristol

Those are useful things for our elected representatives   Well you won't see them debating it on
to be debating.   Monday because there is a bipartisan agree...

Roundtable discussions among high-powered pundits are a staple of contemporary television. Above, the melodious power of Cokie Roberts contrasts with the machine-gun delivery of William Kristol. The words are now coming at two to three times the rate of the truly boring speaker. It's energetic, it's varied, it looks and sounds smart.

Although we've been looking at tonal variation as an element of interest, let's diverge a bit while we're used to looking at spectrograms. Below you see the spectrogram of three very smart people in conversation. Two of them were in a sound studio with good microphones, while one of them was speaking over a telephone. The person on the telephone also sounded slightly angry and defensive. Can you spot the speaker who came across poorly in this broadcast discussion?

| Howard Gardner | Melinda Penkava | E. D. Hirsch |

| *hope that professor Hirsch would agree with that.* | *Well I'd like to put that to E. D. Hirsch. Where do you depart?* | *I'm a very, uh, sort of down to earth...* |

Look at the bottom of the vocal spectrogram of E. D. Hirsch (Mr. Cultural Literacy). The telephone connection has cut off the bottom of his vocal range. His position may have been misrepresented earlier and the tension has raised the pitch of his voice. Even though his voice shows more modulation than Howard Gardner's (Mr. Multiple Intelligences), the high, tinny pitch caused by these circumstances put his ideas at a disadvantage.

| Larry King | Charles Osgood |

| *happy now with the visual form of story telling as you are with the verbal?* | *I still sort of favor radio to tell you the truth. I think the pictures are better.* |

Many professional speakers use their particular set of variations as a trademark. Aside from their intellectual and interpersonal skills, Larry King has a growling voice and wears suspenders, Charles Osgood speaks in soft poetic meter and wears a bow tie.

Taking King's growled last word "verbal" and Osgood's rising, punched first word "I" and stretching the spectrogram for detail, you can see that, as speakers, they are well-differentiated products.

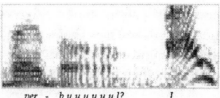

ver - b u u u u u u l?   *I*

Gesture, rate of speech, and tone are just three characteristics that you can vary for interest and expressiveness. Sticking just to your voice for the moment, you have creative control over pitch, volume, rate, resonance, tone. You can take on character voices, even if it's just using a little, teeny voice when you're describing a little, teeny thing. Meaningful vocal variation is the expression of your emotional content rather than an applied decoration. It should not draw attention to itself, by its presence or absence. Habitual patterns, such as a rising tone at the end of every sentence that falsely signals a question ("I'm from Atlanta?"), or overmodulation that is more appropriate for talking to animals and babies, can confuse listeners and give them unnecessary work to do.

Your face is also capable of infinite variation and, just like your voice, you can expand its range by warming it up with exercises. Before making a presentation (if I remember) I try to do "lion and mouse" exercises. Start by opening your eyes and mouth with as big a roaring face as you can muster, and then alternate this with scrunching up as tight as your face and body will go. This exercise is the facial equivalent of singing scales to increase your vocal range.

As Hamlet advised the players, though, you can easily make too much of a good thing: "use all gently . . . Suit the action to the word, the word to the action." I have seen actors who are more interesting to watch when they are just listening than the waving and boisterous generalized expressions of their fellow performers. Still, it's better to have the range of expression available—and not need it—than it is to need it and not have it.

Beyond your constant expressiveness, you can vary discrete parts of the presentation. Find a place where you might sing, ask for audience participation, show a video, offer a game, shift to a demonstration, introduce a new character, tell a story, change locations. Even if you can't find a logical reason to do so, it is better to inject variation arbitrarily than to leave your presentation arbitrarily flat.

It takes a variety of keys to open a variety of locks. The minds of your varied audience are more likely to click open if you draw on a variety of tools. Variation in your presentation ensures that everyone gets a reassuring touch of the familiar, along with exposure to the new. Variation exists not just among individuals but within them as well. For more than 150 years, we have known that human brains are divided into two distinct hemispheres. The left hemisphere is reputedly the home of verbal, analytical, rational, abstract, linear behaviors, and the right hemisphere is home to the visual, holistic, intuitive, concrete, playful behaviors. The two halves of the brain are interconnected and check with one another to reconcile their different perspectives. Together, they enable the high-level learning behaviors of human beings. Although the relationship between the two hemispheres is far more complex, for the sake of ensuring interesting variety, we can consider them an internal "Odd Couple"—a "Bert and Ernie" of the brain.

Traditional, linear, fact-based, analytical education is often accused of fostering a bias against right-brain appeals. Serious learning was considered only that which could be tested with words that represented "the correct answer." This is fine for some subjects, but an extreme left-brain bias might cause you to neglect visual communication. For example, you might struggle to verbally describe a process, without using your hands to actually demonstrate it. The right-brains of your audience will be bored for lack of stimuli. Conversely, an extreme right-brain bias may lead you to neglect facts and figures, names and dates to such a degree that the left-brains of your audience cannot find a "point" to your message.

Since everyone uses both sides of their brain, success often lies in a "multiculturalism for the mind," or a "presentation for both sides of the brain." Knowledge of your own biases can help you be sure that you are making deliberate, professional choices in your

LEFT BRAIN	RIGHT BRAIN
Focuses on **words** ❒	❒ Watches **body language**
Produces **logical** ideas ❒	❒ Produces **humorous** ideas
Prefers **realistic** stories ❒	❒ Prefers **imaginative** stories
Looks for **details** and **facts** ❒	❒ Looks for the **big idea**
Needs **well-structured** tasks ❒	❒ Needs **open-ended** tasks
Learns best from **authorities** ❒	❒ Learns best with **peers**
Solves problems through **logic** ❒	❒ Solves problems **intuitively**
Formal learning environment ❒	❒ **Informal** learning environment
Learns through systematic **plans** ❒	❒ Learning through **exploration**
Solves problems **systematically** ❒	❒ Solves problems **playfully**
Responds to **reasoned** appeals ❒	❒ Responds to **emotional** appeals
Remembers **what** you say ❒	❒ Remembers **how** you say it
Needs **verbal** instructions ❒	❒ Needs **visual** demonstrations
Improves existing things ❒	❒ **Invents** new things
Analytical, then creative ❒	❒ **Creative**, then analytical
Remembers **language** ❒	❒ Remembers **images**
Thinks **sequentially** ❒	❒ Thinks **randomly**
Remembers **names** ❒	❒ Remembers **faces**

work. The folk psychology of left- and right-brain behaviors provides a useful checklist to ensure that you are fully engaging the varied capabilities of the brains around you. You don't need to sacrifice your personality or point of view to achieve "balance"—but neither should force of habit make you inflexibly boring in your appeal. The table above will help you determine if you are neglecting one side or the other.

So if interest is an element of style, the "spice" or the "sizzle," can you neglect the "cake" or the "steak"? Excessive attempts to maintain interest can overwhelm or simply steal too much time from content. But separating substance from style is like dividing mind and body. Interest is not something that is applied to the exterior, but a richness infused in every level. Obviously you have to deliver the principle, the content, as well as the interest.

True interest springs from the thing itself. If the engaging elements of a presentation are disconnected from the content, the focus will be constantly switching back and forth between the two. You must find the elements of interest within your subject and put them to work. Communicators are sometimes seduced by the sound of laughter or the good feeling of personal rapport and easy conversation, and neglect the rest of their job. They develop great technique, but never use it to build anything of significance. They embody the truth that lies at the core of the taunt that you sometimes hear when you're working as a carpenter: "Hey buddy! Are you building something—or just using a hammer?" Just "using your hammer" can be very seductive. Neil Postman worried about this effect in his book *Amusing Ourselves to Death*.

> When a population becomes distracted by trivia, when cultural life is redefined as a perpetual round of entertainments, when serious public conversation becomes a form of baby-talk, when, in short, a people become an audience and their public business a vaudeville act, then a nation finds itself at risk; culture-death is a clear possibility.

Ironically, though, Neil Postman is himself one of the most engaging and entertaining writers around. His technique is as excellent as his message is thought-provoking. We need not worry too much about being excessively interesting. As Kenneth Eble wrote in *The Craft of Teaching*:

> I have seen fewer charlatans than mediocrities and have been less appalled by flashy deception than by undisguised dullness. And I have never encountered any evidence that a dull and stodgy presentation necessarily carries with it an extra measure of truth and virtue.

Chapter 6
Make an Impression

We have always learned best from experience. Say we (Australopithecusly speaking) are walking along our prehistoric streambed looking under rocks for crayfish. Suddenly we turn and see that a wild dog has crept up behind us. Our fight or flight reaction kicks in and as we throw up our arms to make ourselves larger and more threatening, we let go of the rock in our hand and see it land near the wild dog and frighten him off. Now that's useful information—tossing a rock makes the dog go away! With our stress hormones pumping, we remember this experience, so that when a dog approaches us the next day we are reminded of the earlier experience. We throw the rock again, and the dog goes away again. Those of us whose brains make the dog–rock throwing connection will have a better chance of surviving to produce children. If you already have children, and you can tell the story of the rock and the dog to them, they will also gain a survival advantage—if they remember it.

Ever since the first mother showed the first child how to crack open a nut with a rock, ever since the first hunters returned to the cave with news of approaching herds, people have been consciously organizing and passing on information. Informative, dare we say, "educational" communication is a noble realm, between the transitory pleasures of entertainment and the coercive agendas of persuasion.

Remembering a lot of stories and quickly making the best, most useful match to new situations is equivalent to having a lot of experience. We share our stories to strengthen our group and to enhance our status within it. As we age we collect many stories, and if we can match the ones with useful insights to the stories of others, we become the wise ones of our tribe. If everyone has already heard all of our stories, but we keep repeating them, we become a boring old coot.

Passing on wisdom means that it must enter the long-term memory of others. Long-term memory uses two forms of association to keep order, stories and categories. Stories are the episodic memories of places and events. Categories are the semantic collections of concepts and ideas. For example, you probably remember your first car as part of your life story, but you also remember that car as part of the category of all cars. We'll see that these two types of associations, the episodic and the categorical, are the most common forms for informative presentations.

Stories

The wiring in our brains has evolved to take in, learn, and remember an episodic story because it mimics the temporal structure and emotional intensity of direct experience. The act of remembering and retelling the story, of paring it down to the essential information and then reconstructing and elaborating it for retelling, helps us remember it.

If intelligence is overcoming obstacles, then stories are packages of intelligence, because stories show a hero overcoming obstacles to achieve an objective. Because the brain keeps stories and real experiences in separate places, it knows the difference between them as it tries to relate them, but the listeners respond as if the events were actually taking place. One reason we like stories is that they remove the fear of the unknown. Stories, like play, give us the benefit of experience without the risk. Someone has made such a journey as we may face and lived to tell about it, so the mere existence of a story is comforting.

The meaning of a well-told story—with clearly defined characters, a strong plot, and plenty of action—is clear to the listener. A realistic story must be believable within the context of real experience, and even a fantastic story follows the logic of its own set of rules. If the story demands that a magic ring has special powers, you simply agree and the story moves on.

In telling the story, you need clarity, contrast, and definition. The characters must have voices that are sufficiently different that they can readily be told apart. Your hero's allies underscore his or her characteristics. Antagonists define what the protagonist is not. You begin with action, and reveal the characters through their actions. Here is one of my favorites:

> One evening a weary husband returned home early. As he approached his bedroom he heard a frantic scurrying and opened the door just in time to see his wife rearranging her clothes and a man jumping out the window. He looked out the window, but the man was gone. In the dark, he could see that the culprit had left his shoes behind. Turning to his wife, he said, "I am shamed and dishonored. In tomorrow's light I shall see whose shoes lie beneath the window, but now I must sleep in bitter sadness."
>
> As he slept, his wife crept to the window and replaced the interloper's shoes with her husband's own shoes. When the husband awoke the next morning and went to look at the shoes, he saw that they were his own. "Wife! Wife! Wake up!" he cried. "My honor is restored! Look, dear wife, look at the shoes!" he said, proudly holding them up. "It was I who jumped out of the window!"

In good storytelling, dramatic tension rises and falls but relentlessly escalates to a climax. Even in the preceding story, you can break it into three acts. The first act is the setup, showing us the

main character, what they want, and what stands in their way. The audience begins to care and go along, but the act ends with unresolved action to keep the audience hooked. The second act contains the confrontation—overcoming obstacles in the struggle toward the goal with a possible reversal of fortune, and ends with another plot point. Finally, the climax—the point when the action decides for or against the protagonist—forces the resolution. Every action generates a reaction within the constantly shifting environment of the drama, but the overall struggle of the hero remains throughout.

When your audience encounters your new story, they try to benefit from past experience by searching their memory for the best match. That best matching "place" is also where they will store their memories of this new event. For you and your audience to move as a team from their initial state of mind, through the integration of new information, into an enriched state of mind, you each have work to do:

First, you must have something worthwhile to offer.

Which they must see and hear, smell, touch, and taste.

So you must be sure that they can see, hear, etc., clearly.

They must organize this sensory input into packages.

So you use clear, simple, and recognizable language, graphics, and structure.

They must compare the new information to old information.

So you help the process with accurate parallels and analogies.

They must assign meaning to the new information.

So you use clear and concrete associations rather than overly abstract or ambiguous material.

They must store select material in long-term memory.

So you repeat information with variation and multisensory inputs, you chunk and unitize information. You associate emotional stimulation with your message, and you avoid overload.

Having dealt with most of the early steps of this process in previous chapters, and the details of graphics being beyond the scope of this book, we will take up the process at the point of using clear and familiar structures.

Use Clear & Familiar Structures

When you say the four words "Once upon a time . . . ," your audience knows immediately that you are about to fill in a familiar structure. It's like handing them an egg carton before you start handing them the eggs. Cueing your audience to your structure prepares them to lay down the associations and interpret the meaning of your story as it moves through the three stages of setup, conflict, and resolution. These three stages mirror the way in which we learn: from our present state of knowledge, to the confrontation of new knowledge, to integrating a new state of knowledge.

So when you structure your presentations to contain a

Setup .... Confrontation .... Resolution

the most basic episodic patterns are

chronological	beginning	middle	end
spatial	objective & start	journey	finish
process	overview	steps 1, 2, 3, ...	completion

These become more interesting as stories when they are more in line with the three-part mythic structure defined by Joseph Campbell. In the mythic pattern, the hero leaves home and travels to a fantastic land, overcomes powerful forces, and then returns home bringing new powers, or, in short:

mythic	departure.....................	initiation	return

Stories also need a clear direction involving either

growth/increase	initial state...............	improvement	victory
decrease	initial state...............	deterioration	loss

These are story lines where the individual changes. For example, young boxer Rocky grows by making sacrifices and manages to "go the distance"; the Roman Empire falls after becoming self-indulgent and weak. But if the central character steadfastly endures events happening around them, the story is said to be more plot-driven.

steadfastness	initial state..................	challenge	victory / loss

George Washington "cannot tell a lie" and is punished but retains his nobility. George Patton does not adapt to peacetime and is sidelined.

More intellectual structures may also follow the setup-confrontation-resolution pattern

thesis	proposition	proof	conclusion
cause and effect	effect	investigation	cause

or the inherently confrontational pattern

comic	order	disorder	new order
rule and exception	develop rule	exception	new rules
dialectic	thesis	antithesis	synthesis

If the audience is dubious toward you or your proposition, then take them on board with you through structures that give them a step-by-step approach, such as:

problem solving	problem	analysis	solution
two-sided	define issue	pro/con	decision
process of elimination	define need	not this, not this	but this
argument/refutation	problem	dialog	conclusion

For example: "We agree that this intersection is dangerous. Let's look at possible solutions. Evidence shows that a stoplight would be dangerous because of the curve. So we see that the best solution is to reduce the speed limit."

If your audience is already well informed on the subject, acknowledge this but take them into new territory through

order of degree	define category	• • ● or ● • •	summary
common/uncommon	common	uncommon	broader view
familiar/strange	familiar	unfamiliar	commonality

or search for relationships and patterns through inductive or deductive patterns.

inductive   introduce issue ... compare specifics .... derive rule

For example: This approach worked here, it worked here, and it worked here, it should work everywhere. Or

deductive   general .... specific case .... conclusion

as in: All men are mortal, Socrates is a man, Socrates is mortal.

Although these approaches have wandered away from the purely informative into the realm of the persuasive (the next chapter), we might as well go all the way with two of the full-tilt emotional appeals.

strengthening belief   ! .... !! .... !!!
call to action   belief .... warrant .... action

Finally, if nothing else will keep you from rambling, narrow the topic down to manageable highlights.

important elements   pre-summary .... A, B, C .... summary

There is no reason to think that the universe actually behaves according to these structures, and we often distort reality to make it conform to these thematic forms. We say, "What's the story here?" when in fact there may be no story—the events may have transpired without clear direction—therefore we impose direction in order to meet some internal need for such packaging. Our minds seem to like this kind of order because they mimic and economically package the interesting neural paths of direct experience.

The overall structure gives clarity to the whole, but a presentation of any length will use a variety of substructures woven into it.

The substructures offer variety and enable you to make the middles more interesting. Because people more easily remember beginnings (the primacy factor) and the ending (recency), important material in the middle needs to come in its own little interesting packages. Like having scene changes in a long play, shortening the distances between beginnings and endings helps those hardworking brains to package and store your information.

Categories + Associations + Feelings = Meaning

Your audience is always learning, always processing information, always trying to make mental order out of the stimuli that you present. Their brains are conservative organs, though, and will compare all new information with older information already in place. In addition to wanting to assemble information in familiar ways, they will try to interpret the meaning of your information to confirm their current beliefs. Everyone sees the world through their own pair of glasses.

Meaninglessness or the misperception of meaning is an unintended result of the problem-solving process. When you speak and move, the audience works to find a meaning for your behavior, trying to make complete pictures long before your words are complete. They may be way ahead of you in deciding what you mean.

It is useless to argue over meaning, as if it were a property of the word or symbol itself. All we can do is explain our perceptions and associations. A traumatic experience with something may give it meaning for one person that is not commonly shared by others. Ohio State and Kent State Universities have shared categories, but for many people of a certain age, they have distinctly different emotional meanings. When we successfully communicate our intended meaning to another person, we say we have had a meaningful conversation. Still, each individual has their own perception of your intention.

Their Perception = Their Reality
Your Perception ≠ Their Perception

Each person has their individual sensory experience to which they ascribe meaning, which, in turn, triggers associated emotional responses. Your words and actions trigger their memories: first of categories, then associations, then their feelings. We provide a "meaningful experience" for people when we trigger numerous coherent feelings. We try to communicate our intended meaning by stimulating the intended associations within the other person beyond the level of literal meaning to *affective* meaning. We succeed when they "get it" in their own way, but a way that is still close to our own.

The mind also tends to economize. We tend to perceive and remember the simpler explanation rather than the complex. This is why people try to "peg" you. Even when looking at a picture, our scanning vision comes to rest on corners and angles. We record these in the brain to define a complete picture for later recall. When we study history we see the battles and crises—again we are picking out the corners, the great turning points of history. In history, as in the visual arts as well as drama, we have the strongest attraction to the point at which change occurs. The "pause for emphasis" and other highlighting techniques define the corners for the audience to use. The brain seizes on them to economically reconstruct the points in between.

Understanding and reconstructing are easier if we can fit the new information into preexisting categories. As we saw earlier, many presenters try to put familiar labels on unfamiliar items to aid understanding, to help make it "relate to the lives of the audience." When the automobile first appeared, we were faced with a new thing and called it by a combination of old things, a horseless carriage. This is a useful behavior that eases us through the transition until the new idea takes hold. But in this labeling, the words are straining

The same message triggers many responses.
(adapted from Deirdre Johnston, 1994)

to describe a new reality, and they tie our minds to the old understanding.

Labeling also shapes our memory. If I were to show you this picture (and tell you it was a picture of the moon, when asked to recall it some time later you would tend to "correct" the memory to make it look more like this image ((which is more in line with the concept of a crescent moon than the original. If, however, I had told you it was a crab claw, your recalled drawing would tend to look more like this ⊂. If you try to make the unfamiliar familiar by labeling it, remember the price you pay. Labeling reality with a mismatched concept distorts your audience's recall to make it better comply with the label. People will tend to see and remember what you tell them to see and remember. Things are what they are, they can often be understood as they are.

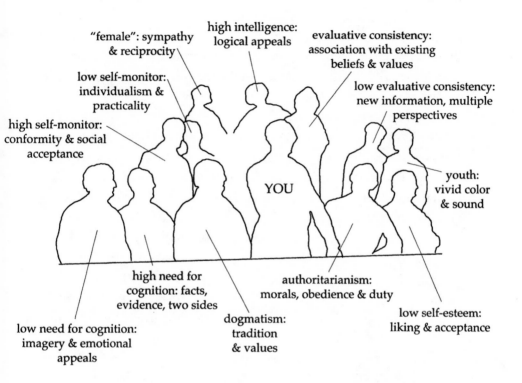

"female": sympathy & reciprocity

high intelligence: logical appeals

evaluative consistency: association with existing beliefs & values

low self-monitor: individualism & practicality

low evaluative consistency: new information, multiple perspectives

high self-monitor: conformity & social acceptance

YOU

youth: vivid color & sound

high need for cognition: facts, evidence, two sides

authoritarianism: morals, obedience & duty

low self-esteem: liking & acceptance

low need for cognition: imagery & emotional appeals

dogmatism: tradition & values

So, if you want to make a specific impression on a wide variety of people, use concrete examples, not abstract ones. If you want to stimulate a wider variety of interpretations, use a more abstract presentation, giving more control of the interpretation of meaning to the audience. But it is the work of the audience to get the parallels of the story to their own lives. If you have told the story well, they will in turn offer their interpretation of the meaning. If you have to explain the parallels, you are both insulting the audience and admitting that you are unskilled at your craft.

Comparisons stink, but children have a smaller data bank of experiences. Everything is new and may be bewildering until linked to their smaller data set. The problem comes when you misjudge the need of the audience for your metaphor. I once heard a radio reporter interviewing another reporter on the emerging, horrific details of the "killing fields" of the Khmer Rouge in Cambodia. For the benefit of her listeners, she tried to clarify the other reporter's graphic descriptions of Pol Pot's deliberate starvation of millions of Cambodians as "sort of a let them eat *rice* cake approach." If the genocide had occurred in South America, would she similarly have aided our understanding by calling it a "let them eat *corn* cake approach"? This is help no one needs.

Which brings us back to reading feedback to check for comprehension and to allow you to follow the interest of the audience. When the size of the audience permits, take questions as you go along rather than making them wait until the end. Keep your eyes on your audience so you can try a new analogy if the first one fails, or remember not to use it the next time. You have a plan, a path, but you also have a responsibility to constantly search for a better one.

Informational content is often just the vehicle for the real meaning. The manner of a presentation may well carry more weight than the "declarative" meaning. If you talk down to, alienate, and distance people, your meaning is clear. If you let your audience actively participate in constructing meaning, you show that you have taken them on as working partners and they have accepted you as a leader.

Use Repetition

It takes time for your audience to store information in

long-term memory. Memory is a biochemical process, not a purely electrical one. Neurons need time to strengthen the pathways of memory. Repetition also keeps information present long enough for us to find out what associations to store it with. Simple repetition of a key idea strengthens recall—up to the point of three repetitions before diminishing returns set in. Repetition is too often a crude and oppressive tool—overused because it works. Introductions and summaries that are too similar to the body of your message become the stultifying, "tell 'em what you're going to tell 'em, tell 'em, and tell 'em what you told 'em" approach. Skillfully used, it does not have to be such a blunt club. (How about "show 'em what you're going to show 'em" or "smell 'em what you're going to tell 'em"?) Spread the repetitions throughout the presentation, rather than bunching

them up, and vary the approach. It is not the broken record approach, but repetition well distributed with variety, which makes the greatest impression.

Repetition without variation gives you boring programs like one I saw attempting to present dramatically the reactions of different members of an antebellum household to the impending death of the patriarch. In the first scene we met a slave concerned that she might be sold, in the second scene we met a political ally concerned with the power implications, in the third scene we met the widow concerned with having to make it on her own.

"Now to help you imagine what Odysseus must have smelled like at this point in his journey."

Although their reasons for concern were all *factually* different, they were *dramatically* identical; each of the three monologues resonated with our single internal story of the anxiety we feel when facing uncertainty. The emotional content was repeated three times, and the result was deadly. As one of the audience members commented on the way out, "I think these people needed to be alone."

Problem solving (one of the seven elements of interest from the previous chapter) also compels the audience to do repetitions. You can select any point on a gradient from simple to complex tasks. Ask for recognition: "So which is the right gasket for this cylinder head?" Ask for specific recall: "Remember when we saw the flow meter? What was the most important thing in accuracy?" or general recall: "What struck you the most? Did you see any connections between . . . ?" Ask your audience to recall information, to show that they understand, to apply their new knowledge, to analyze how the knowledge was acquired, to synthesize new ideas, to evaluate the experience and concepts. This is the chance for them to find the relevance to their own lives. It is also a chance to repeat.

Use Multisensory Inputs

You may have discovered that taking notes in a class helped you remember the important material, even if you never looked at the notes again. The more of our senses that we use while learning, the more redundant the pathways in the brain, the better we learn. In listening and writing we use dual coding. Recalling something we only heard is only single-coded and may not be remembered as accurately. Using the multisensory appeals in your presentation makes your message more memorable.

Your five human senses bring you different amounts of information. Ruth Schwarze in *The Science of Creativity* apportions perception by the senses in this way:

3% through tasting
3% through smelling
3% through touching
13% through hearing
78% through seeing

This only accounts for information coming into our perception. But change happens only if the new information is retained in our memory to shape our behavior later on. Schwarze further states that we remember:

20% of what we hear
40% of what we see

Educational authority William Lewis observed that people retain about:

10% of what they hear
30% of what they read
50% of what they see
90% of what they do

To hear a good lecture is an inspiring experience. We leave with our imagination broadened and our interest piqued; we find ourselves entertained, prodded, and illuminated in turn. What evokes our response is an intricate blend of qualities. The lecture must have sufficient intellectual content to challenge us, and enough clarity of exposition that we are not left disoriented and confused. Like a dramatic monologue, it engages our emotions and keeps them in play, thanks to frequent shifts in mood and intensity. It mixes humor and erudition, and gives us a sense of the personal involvement of the lecturer in his or her topic. It reassures us as well by providing a small island of coherence in an often chaotic world. These elements, taken together, create a series of inner tensions that give life to the lecture. The result may be difficult to define, but is instantly recognizable.

Heather Dubrow and James Wilkinson, *The Art and Craft of Teaching*

Schwarze and Lewis are in rough agreement—seeing is at least twice as effective as hearing. It's good advice then, to "show" your subject, rather than just "tell" about it. It's a bad idea, however, to treat any of these senses and behaviors in isolation. They all work in concert to enable people to reach understanding. That is the strength of presenting a demonstration to make your point. It is a multisensory, concrete example of the big idea.

Lewis adds a curious category, "what they do," to his table. Hearing is doing. Reading is doing. Seeing is doing. The "doing" difference is active engagement rather than passive intake. "Doing" goes by many names; it's called activity, participation, constructivism, involvement, inquiry, hands on, minds on, active listening, interaction, etc. Most often, communicators use verbal instructions to direct the learners to do active, memorable things. Remember the old proverb:

> If you tell me—I will forget.
> If you show me—I will remember.
> If you let me do it—I will understand.

Changing locations is another strong adjunct to memory recall. Obviously, remembering where something happened is important to our survival. If everything happens in the same place for your audience, they may not have enough "hooks" for the memories. New information is often associated with moving into a new space in the brain. Everyone remembers where they were when they first heard "the news."

The teacher who lets students learn by experiment is also teaching them that they are capable of determining the nature of reality for themselves. Anything that actively involves the audience, such as getting them to sum up or apply the subject matter, improves the memory of that subject. Thus we have "Repeat after me" and "So what are you going to do the next time you . . . ?" When a visitor to a corporate headquarters hears "Can anyone translate that Latin motto on the crest above the door?" they are no longer just hearing at a 10 percent retention rate, now they are doing so at a 90 percent retention rate.

These percentages need to be taken with a big grain of salt. How can we really measure information intake and retention so precisely? Still, the principle bears the test of folk wisdom.

> "In one ear and out the other."
>> "A picture is worth a thousand words."
>>> "Actions speak louder than words."

Once Bitten Twice Shy — Emotions & Memory

Most of us have persistent emotional memories that we would like to forget if we could. These persistent memories, some reaching far back into our childhood, are related to experiences that stimulated our "fight or flight" response. In addition to releasing adrenaline and sugars into our bloodstream so that we can respond to the threat, this neurochemical response helped fix the associated events into our long-term memory.

Again, the survival advantage of this phenomenon is obvious. Animals that remember where they were attacked are more likely to have surviving offspring. Fortunately, emotional stimulation also helps us remember details surrounding positive events as well. Discover a treasure under the floorboards and you will remember. Given a limited capacity for storage and retrieval, it is important that we have a mechanism to help us remember what is important.

This connection between emotion and memory also works with adrenaline doses below the heart-pounding-running-to-escape-the-sabertoothed-tiger level. It works proportionally. Good news or an insult at the office will trigger a release of hormones and intensify memory. Watching an effective dramatic presentation or hearing a good story triggers emotional responses and enhances memory. Games and competition enhance memory. In early medieval times, when memory was predominant over writing, children were given presents (or occasionally burned!) so that they would remember

witnessing a transaction. Scholars of the same period memorized lengthy texts by "tagging" key parts with funny stories and naughty rhymes. Thus, if the information is important for your audience to remember, find a way to associate it with an emotional response.

Scientific and other esoteric presentations particularly benefit from backing off at the beginning to link up with the bigger, human-interest picture. An emotionally engaging opening view in a highly specialized presentation can supply an emotional context for the details that follow. Even though the audience can follow the information without this emotional element, it will still help them remember it. Painter Norman Rockwell reportedly admitted that if a painting wasn't working, he would put a puppy in it. If it still wasn't working, he would put a bandage on the puppy's paw.

As Dr. James McGaugh, a leading researcher into this phenomenon said, "The advice to the teacher would be to embed the information you want the children to learn in an emotionally exciting context. And there'll be a higher probability that this information will be remembered and used. There's nothing wrong with that."

Or is there? You may recall Parson Weems whose history books included such tales as George Washington and the cherry tree. Young Washington, the perfect man, was so good that he could not tell a lie, and took his punishment rather than blame the crime on someone else. An unforgettable tale of honesty—one that is in itself a lie. A real figure from history has been moved into the realm of myth. The benefit is memory, the cost is truth.

Toward the end of the nineteenth century, German educational reformers also tried to make history more engaging. They advocated more storytelling and emotional appeals. In 1925, one former student recalled his response to this new method. "My teacher, by the fire of his words, sometimes made us forget the present; as if by magic, he transported us into times past, . . . and transformed dry historical facts into vivid reality. . . . This teacher made history my favorite subject." The student was Adolf Hitler. The power of the emotional appeal is there for good or evil.

Avoid Overload

Overload of new information interferes with memory. Adding new, but similar, information can crowd out the memory of the earlier material. A list of dates is terribly hard to remember because they are too much alike. Lists of distinctly different items like chickens, Detroit, 1721, and bongos are easier to recall. Here's where it helps you to know what the audience has been through before you get them. If they have been exposed to volumes of similar information earlier in the day, you would be wise to shift gears.

Have realistic expectations about passing on information. Be content with the three to five big "take-home" ideas. Even an interested audience will forget most of your presentation within a week. Your audience will not remember everything you present, but they must get the basic message and the desire and process to learn more. Many things cannot be taught but can only be learned, so if you can spark an interest and show a process that will allow them to find out what they need, then you have done your job. And if you have done it well, they will come back to you.

Because endings are easier to remember, most informative presentations end with a recapitulation of the middle information through examples, highlights, a summary, or an overt statement of the moral message or logical implications of the story. There is nothing wrong with this practice, as long as it does not become a substitute for audience engagement and comprehension throughout the presentation—mere repetition. Instead of tying up all the loose ends in a neat package so the audience can stop thinking, leave an agent at work, gnawing into their brains. A thoughtful question, a moving quotation, an inspiring challenge—but most of all, don't make it too far from the beginning.

CHAPTER 7
CREATE A CONVICTION

E very thinking person is an ongoing construction project. Some of their structure is made from beliefs, ideas considered to be true or false with varying degrees of certainty. Alongside the beliefs are attitudes, which are emotional positions ranging from liking through disliking. The beliefs and attitudes are built on a foundation of fundamental values. These values, attitudes, and beliefs may be as varied as a sense of fairness, a dislike of turnips, and belief in a rational world. Some are superficial, but some go very deep, and these, along with fundamental values, are the lowest bricks in the wall and the hardest to move. In a harmonious construction, the values, attitudes, and beliefs support one another in a useful and pleasing whole. There may be tension, compression, or torsion, but the center holds. Until you come along.

You come along and, having examined the structure, point out a weakness or discover a missed opportunity. You propose a new bit of work, one that will remedy the fault, one that will be more useful, one that will increase comfort, all to the advantage of the individual. They have the power to make the change that you propose, but you generate the motivation for them to undertake it.

The new construction must fit in with the old—aesthetically, logically—and this is the paradoxical key to changing beliefs—with maximum consistency. The more things *seem* to stay the same the more easily they change. Even when we do question one of our beliefs, we look only for reasons to support it, not for reasons against it. Therefore, the more consistent you can make your objective appear with someone's goals, attitudes, values, and beliefs, the easier it will be for them to adopt your new view. This consistency involves

the whole person—their feelings, their identity, their construction of reality, not just their understanding of the facts, as in this version of the story of Napoleon and the plea for mercy:

A young soldier in Napoleon's army was facing execution for desertion in the face of the enemy. His mother managed to gain an audience with the emperor to beg that he spare her son. Napoleon rebuffed her pleas.

"Your son ran and left others to fight and die. Justice demands that your son pay for his cowardice."

"But excellency," she replied, "I do not ask for justice, I ask for mercy."

"Your son does not deserve mercy."

"Excellency, if he *deserved* mercy, it would not *be* mercy."

And with that, Napoleon pardoned the son.

What made Napoleon change his mind? The mother agreed that her son was guilty, and asserted that mercy went only to the undeserving. She won only a small semantic point— but that was enough. For Napoleon not to concede the game after the mother won her point would have been ignoble—entirely inconsistent with his core values of honor and majesty. To maintain

his consistency with the rest of his values and attitudes, he had to change his belief in the necessity for justice. *Plus c'est la même chose, plus ça change.*

William James described this path-of-least-resistance using a horticultural metaphor. "The individual has a stalk of old opinions already, but he meets a new experience that puts them to a strain. The result is an inward trouble, to which his mind, till then, had been a stranger, and from which he seeks to escape by modifying his previous mass of opinions. At least some new idea comes up which he can graft upon the ancient stalk with a minimum of disturbance of the latter. Some idea that mediates between the stalk and the new experience and runs them into one another most felicitously and expeditiously, this new idea is then adopted as the true one."

Dissonance, this "inward trouble," if not so strong as to be repellent, is engaging. Generating dissonance gets internal and external dialog going. One of the bricks in the wall is starting to give, it's beginning to wriggle loose. Planting the seeds of discontent also gives your proposal a dynamic, dramatic tension to draw in your audience. I often work with groups of medical scientists to improve their skills in teaching, lecturing, and presenting papers. Early in the workshop, I will ask: "What is more important, neuroscience or cheerleading? Neuroscience or middle school football? Neuroscience or ROTC close order drill?" The audience, all neuroscientists, of course affirm that they value neuroscience above these other endeavors, but they know something is coming. I then ask them to explain why, if they believe their work is more important, do cheerleaders, athletes, and military cadets regularly videotape, study, and strive to improve their presentations, and neuroscientists do not? "Is your work with students, patient groups, and your fellow scientists less important?" The inconsistency provokes thought, dialog, a searching examination of their interconnected structure of values, attitudes, beliefs, and behaviors. They have moved from complacent to questioning, questioning generates dialog, and dialog is a step toward change.

As the persuader, you provoke the inward trouble—but you can't just be a troublemaker, you also must lead to the remedy. You show how you understand the problem and offer a solution—your proposal, your proposition. You engage your empathy to help you to see things as they do so your solution will fit. My audience of scientists explains the demands on their time. How can they sacrifice time from substance and give it over to style? They are dedicated to producing more matter and less art. I listen, and through discussion, we agree if time is the problem, then all the more reason to develop good presentation habits that will make better communication automatic and that will give their scientific labors more impact. You have to show that you understand the difficulty of their situation, and frame your solution to fit it.

You want something, but they have the power of choice. What will they get in return for making the choice your way? You can make the change as easy and profitable as possible, but if it goes against a core value, against one of those bottom bricks, the cost may be too great. Just as you are well advised to question your own long-held beliefs, you will have a hell of a time getting others to question theirs. Rarely can you persuade someone to do something

Challenges to our fundamental values seldom open people to change.

inconsistent with their deepest held values because they are the foundations of their reality, personality, and identity.

Values, such as our taboo on cannibalism, are deeply, culturally embedded. Attitudes, beliefs, and behaviors are more varied in their mobility, but are still subject to inertia. When our beliefs are challenged, we will either try to shut out the challenge, try to attack the credibility or motives of the source, or try to interpret the message so that it fits better with our preexisting beliefs, or, rarest and hardest of all, we may change.

When we do change, we must find some means of supporting the change, just as when we act inconsistently with our attitudes, we must rationalize the inconsistency. We have a core value not to take human life, but support killing in warfare by developing beliefs that dehumanize, and attitudes that make us hate the enemy. If we abandon previously liberal beliefs, we say it is because we were mugged. We need logical validation for the emotional position, and our intellect willingly provides a rational fig leaf to conceal our embarrassing animal drives.

Motivating or Manipulating?

This persuasion business is getting ethically messy already. Again, recall what the twentieth century's guru of glad-handing, Dale Carnegie, said: "The best argument is that which *seems* merely an explanation." His use of the word "seems" reveals the deceptive nature of much persuasion. Forewarned is forearmed in resisting change, so there is an incentive to disguise persuasion, to slip it in unannounced. Too often persuasion has been the art of disengaging the intelligence of others to serve selfish ambition and avarice. It is too painfully obvious that persuasion is often used to exploit others. One is tempted just to say, "I will not attempt to persuade, I will just let the facts speak for themselves."

But this too is folly, because it assumes everyone perceives data and interprets it the same as you. They don't.

One of many ways people differ is in their ability to see the trees for the forest. Have you ever noticed that some people seem to be "luckier" than others in finding sharks' teeth on a beach or arrowheads in a plowed field? This is caused by differences in people's dependence on the perceptual background or field. People with a strong field dependence are more distracted by the background; those who tend to ignore the background are field independent—and can find the needle faster.

This aspect of personality affects more than just ability to discern hidden pictures. Henry David Thoreau, who could look down and find an arrowhead just about anywhere he stood, also had the other patterns of strong field independence—he was a self-reliant thinker with little need for social cues to guide his perceptions. His view from the edge helped the rest of the population see things they had never seen before. Our vision has been extended by his persuasive writings. But, of course, Thoreau was not a "people-person" and would have made a lousy politician. This job calls for the field-dependent individual who thrives in social situations—someone more tuned in to personal relationships than in to isolated concepts. People can work together from the two extremes for the greater good, and they often need to persuade each other to consider their alternate point of view, as in the following episode from my own adventures in management.

An executive manager at our museum village had all the characteristics of a strongly field-dependent cognitive style. He was well-liked by everyone, a great mixer and socializer with strong social relationships throughout the organization. This is a great strength in an organization that depends on donors. True, field-dependent people can be more prone to deception by skilled manipulators but, overall, he did a fine job. When it came to isolating conceptual problems though, welllll . . . here's an example.

On busy days lines formed at smaller sites in our village. The management response had always been to tell public-contact people to speed up their presentations so that the lines would move faster. But this never worked, because (counterintuitively) speeding up the presentations just put people back on the street to join another line at another site. The problem, isolated by computer-modeling, was one not of time, but of space. The answer was not, for example, to get the shoemakers to speed up their presentation, but to have one

of them move outside under their shed and thus increase the audience capacity of their site. If every other site in the village did something similar, the capacity of the museum could expand to meet demand. The lines would go away. Simple.

But it never happened, because I failed to persuade the executive manager to change the policy. I relied on the "facts" and ignored cognitive style. I presented the computer animations, the spreadsheets, and even a demonstration where we moved around golf balls representing visitors between different-sized coffee cans representing the sites in the village. It should have worked, but although the executive manager saw the individual "proofs," he looked to the others in the room to see how they felt about the matter. Of course they were all his subordinates and were in turn looking to him for cues before they voiced an opinion. Stalemate.

In retrospect, I should have approached all the other managers first and shown them the data, relying on their numbers to represent an average degree of field dependence/independence. Once the management group was convinced and committed, they would in turn provide the social proof that the executive manager needed for him to be convinced to change the policy. It's like putting the value of pi to a vote, but *vive la différence*. We need each other to see things we can't and sometimes that calls for persuasion, not information. If people responded only to data, we could have ended with the last chapter, but people just don't see things the same way. Persuasion respects the reality of human diversity.

Audience Diversity

Audiences as groups are as different as individuals. Just as in informing them, persuading begins where the audience is intellectually and emotionally. You must understand and acknowledge your audience's fundamental reality and build your case upon the foundations that are already in place. These may be the basic human needs, "We all want to provide for our families . . . ," basic values of

Logical arguments seldom convert those who are already committed.

fairness, honor, or even disagreeable prejudices. Make the emotional, fundamental alignment with their values, attitudes, and beliefs, backing up to just before the point of divergence, leaving any logical reasoning until you need it to cover over any cracks in the final construction.

Different audiences demand different approaches. You have to work even more at the emotional level if you want to provoke change in a diverse audience. Even if mass audiences are able to follow a sophisticated logical argument, it may not persuade them. Although you can throw in a logical argument to deflect scrutiny from an emotional position, logic by itself will rarely change a diverse audience. Demagogues have long learned to provoke unified beliefs from the masses by appeals to common emotional responses. Even with our educated citizenry, we are more consistent in our responses generated by fear, greed, hunger, and need for self-esteem than in our response to intellectual and logical issues.

The other end of the scale is an audience that is already highly informed about a subject, say, a scientific discipline, where the rules of logical behavior are highly developed. So where is your audience?

Is your audience .... *diverse* .... or ......*homogenous?*
ignorant .... or .... *informed?*
opinionated ..... or .... *open?*
distant .... or .... *proximal?*

Will your new idea be .. *dissonant* .... or .... *consistent?*

Because that
determines whether
your strategy can be ..... *emotional* .... or .... *logical*
simple .... or .... *complex*

Of course you have to combine both emotional and logical appeals, but the wrong emphasis can seem far out of place. Every group has its conventions and expectations about the acceptable balance of the two. Some disciplines separate emotion and logic to an excessive degree. Sherlock Holmes said that romanticizing the science of detection is like "working a love-story into the fifth proposition of Euclid." Still, well-balanced individuals respond to both, so use a range of persuasive appeals on both the rational and emotional sides. You can say that the "thinkers" will need the logic, and the "feelers" will need the emotion, but in truth, everyone needs both.

If you have to educate your audience about a subject in order to be persuasive, it will simply take longer. Environmentalist Rachel Carson was able to educate, persuade, and change the world with her book *Silent Spring*. Conversely, intellectual downsizing, appealing to the baser instincts of the audience, follows William Burroughs's observation that it is easier to degrade your customers than to improve your product. In *All the King's Men*, a frustrated campaign aide finally tells failing candidate Willie Stark how to succeed:

> You tell 'em too much . . . Hell, make 'em cry, make 'em laugh, . . . make 'em mad. Even mad at you. Just stir 'em up, it doesn't matter how or why, and they'll love you and come back for more . . . It's up to you to give 'em something to stir 'em up and make 'em feel alive again. Just for half an hour. That's what they come for. Tell 'em anything. But for Sweet Jesus' sake don't try to improve their minds.

This is the strategy of the demagogue: Progressively disengage intelligence by making base emotional appeals covered with a thin candy shell of logic.

Demagogues may not try to improve people's minds, but they must know them. So must you. To persuade, you must be sure that

you know their real concerns. Say you are in a discussion about which route to take up a mountain. If you argue in favor of route B on the basis that it is faster than route A, you might succeed if speed is the decision factor for your fellow traveller. If, however, unbeknownst to you, they are only concerned with the scenic merits of the competing routes, your argument about the fastest route will be unpersuasive, if not counterproductive. Should you uncover the secret preference for the scenic route, you might agree to it, or you might argue for the scenic qualities of your preferred route and that arriving at the location sooner will give you more time to look around before dark. When a reasoned argument fails to persuade, you may need to dig for the real issue.

But why do you have to dig? Why would someone keep you in the dark about their true motivations? Sometimes they themselves don't know, but more often, I believe, agendas stay hidden because the truth would be embarrassing. No one wants to reveal motivations based on personal fear, greed, ambition, or affections that run against the goals of the group. This may be why, as Henry Kissinger observed, academic politics are so vicious "because the stakes are so low." In nonprofit organizations, the only way to get ahead is by empire-building. This leaves an embarrassing secret power agenda under every debate. Conversations become more authentic and sabotage less likely when there is a clear, common goal—when everyone has an authentic stake in the success of the group.

Sometimes it takes an external threat (real or imagined) to bring people together. Walter Lord observed this in his book on the attack on Pearl Harbor. With ships overturned and burning; with strafing, bombing and torpedoing; with thousands of men burned, injured, or drowning, the rigid hierarchy and the petty rules disappeared. Interviewing the Americans who survived and fought back and worked to save one another, the survivors all "agree that it was a day when rank was forgotten, . . . when people only wanted to pitch in together, . . . when all that counted was the good idea."

When all that counted was the good idea. Imagine.

Choose Your Audience

Choosing your audience sounds like the advice for longevity, "choose your parents well," but it is a common strategy, even outside of the obvious case of jury selection. Long-held beliefs have the advantage of primacy—that which was first believed is most deeply believed, so one audience to choose is the audience of beginners. Try to get in the first shot, the first representation of reality. Within an institution, you will engineer change faster if you can reach newly hired employees rather than waiting until they have been shaped by a year or two on the job. As the manipulative schoolteacher liked to say, "Give me a child at an impressionable age and she is mine for life." You can more easily create and strengthen beliefs and opinions when you begin with a clean slate. Youth and newcomers are such.

The power of primacy applies not just to your verbal statements, but to the complete impression you make on the audience when they first meet you. Within minutes, if not seconds, they will know how they feel about you, so play some of your strongest cards first. If you can't get in your shot at the beginning, you might try to create a new beginning just for you. I have seen clever lawyers, when it comes their turn to speak, look at the court, and with a big show of empathy, ask for a brief adjournment for the sake of the dutiful yet fatigued citizens. If they can get it, they will then try to get in a "brief statement" before the break (a recency advantage during the break) and will then be able to recommence afterwards with the advantage of primacy.

Another easy audience is one that is already pointed in the direction you want them to go. Cheerleaders build on the beliefs of their own side rather than attempting to reason with fans of the opposing team. Cheerleaders just change the intensity of previously held feelings and beliefs, but you can still use their approach to make change in others. Find the sympathetic individuals within the larger group and build your strength upon them, celebrating the values, identity, and accomplishments of the group, lauding their noble ideals. Proclaim their goals in memorable catchphrases. Flatter them and give them tools that strengthen their ability and desire to influence others. Preach to the converted, building your strength with your allies before moving on to more resistant territory.

A strategy that can replace or accompany raising your peasant army is to go right to the top. If persuading a diverse audience is difficult, simply reduce the audience number to one. Find the decision maker who can make the others follow along and structure your appeal directly to them. This puts all your money on one card, of course, and a first refusal makes people less prone to cooperate later on. Still, it is a gamble many are willing to take. Throughout time charlatans, Rasputin types, have swarmed around the powerful, playing to their insecurity. But just because the unscrupulous use this strategy doesn't mean you cannot use it as well.

If you do choose to go to the top, or deal with anyone having the upper hand in power, status, or bargaining position, the "foot in the door" approach is a useful tool. If you can get someone to do a small favor for you, they will be more likely to do progressively larger favors later on. Establish their self-image as "helpful" people and they will tend to maintain consistency with that identity. Making people feel powerful creates in them a responsibility to make things right, and making them feel fortunate makes them feel more like sharing. Leaving a restaurant one evening I encountered a man in a wheelchair at a curb cut, apparently struggling with what should have been an easy ascent to the sidewalk.

"Excuse me, sir, I don't mean to bother you, but could you please help me get up this hill?"

I helped him of course, but as soon as he thanked me, it came.

"Sir? Sir? I don't mean to bother you, you've been so helpful and all, but you see, I need some money to get a cab back to . . ."

He planted the "good and helpful" person image in my head and I had to maintain consistency by subsequently giving him money. If they can get you to salute a flag one week, you are more likely to fight for it the following week. It is the manipulation woven into the fabric of everyday life.

A Favorable Attitude — Make the Audience Like You

People like and trust people similar to themselves. Simply complimenting your audience aligns you with their beliefs—they think well of themselves, and your compliments establish the first point of agreement. If you should mention that you once disagreed with them but have come around to their point of view, they will feel even better, because their position is reconfirmed and they believe that *they* are the persuasive ones.

Management types occasionally try to fake similarity with an audience of subordinates by making gestures at common experience—spending an hour on the customer service lines. This usually comes across as condescending, but, if they frame the experience as an eye-opener, it should work better. For example:

"A week ago I thought we had enough computer capacity. I had heard complaints about how the database slowed down during the busy season, but I never realized how frustrating it was until I spent an hour down there myself. I am amazed at the ingenious ways many of you have discovered to work around the overload."

This gambit flatters the audience—they were justified in their complaints and ingenious in their solutions. The news that they are not getting new computers might now be better accepted. As Lao Tsu observed:

> In order to weaken, one will surely strengthen first.
> In order to overthrow, one will surely exalt first.
> In order to take, one will surely give first.

One of the things to give is help. If others perceive you as a helpful ally, you will be more persuasive. Remember the basic human need to reduce uncertainty. In a new situation, there is tremendous bonding with the person who helps you first "learn the ropes." Lawyers jockey to be the first to explain the unfamiliar courtroom proceedings to the jury—for they will remain in the jury's minds as the helpful person who reduced their uncertainty.

If this kind of manipulation seems unfair, consider the unfairness of physical beauty. Attractive people simply have an easier time of it. As Shakespeare wrote: "Beauty itself doth of itself persuade the eyes of men without an orator." The exception to this is if you evoke jealousy, but most of us are not at risk if we simply look our

best. People are more easily persuaded by those they like than by those they dislike, and people like attractive people.

Over time, attractiveness reaches beneath the skin. A lifetime of positive interactions initiated by good looks builds social skills and self-confidence. Charisma is thus associated with good looks, but it is not the same thing. Personality, intelligence, empathy, and humor all add to charisma, and charisma trumps logic any day.

Although the Greek root of the word "charisma" implies that it is a "divine gift," at least the empathic element of it can be acquired by practice. A charismatic leader constantly monitors the reactions of others—just as the persuasive person is a good listener, a close observer, and an empathic responder. They also count on continuous feedback from trusted colleagues. If your ally whispers to you to lighten up and not be so defensive during a discussion, listen to them. Attorney Gerry Spence always tries to have a colleague in the court keeping tabs on the mood of the room, giving him constant updates. An egocentric approach to persuasion rarely succeeds.

Empathy helps you understand, engage, and shape the moment-by-moment status of others. Highly empathic people can succeed—not on the basis of their ideas, but on their ability to pander to others by insidious chameleonlike mirroring of posture, language, and eye movements. This intense mirroring, beyond the normal, social mirroring, is similar to relationships between mothers and babies. It seems creepy to the outside observer, but its seductive power is as effective as it is primal. It is a deliberate sacrifice of the small things of self to gain control of others.

Leaders inspire others by controlling themselves, taking time to cultivate and maintain the consistency of their image. This is a fully committed form of persuasion, used by persons such as Mohandas Gandhi, Dr. King, or St. Joan who lead in deed as well as word. Prison or other forms of isolation seem a common experience for leaders to develop their persona through self-reflection. During his 27 years in prison, Nelson Mandela had time to develop his objective self-awareness to mirror and refine his self-presentation as a strong moral leader. Mandela gave his followers elevated identity through example and inspiring words such as:

> There's nothing enlightened about shrinking so that other people won't feel insecure around you. We were born to make manifest the glory of God that is within us. It's not just in some of us; it's in everyone. And as we let our own light shine, we unconsciously give other people permission to do the same. As we are liberated from our own fear, our presence automatically liberates others.

These are the words of the strong poet, and his recognition of his own power comes through in the final lines. Eventually his fellow prisoners and even the guards came to look at him as the moral touchstone for their own reality. Mandela was cultivating the attitude of the leader, one who should be imitated and yet still held above others.

Sometimes, though, you just have to turn the job over to somebody they already like. This can be hard on you; you can win all the logical points you want, but if they don't like you, you're dead. Marcia Clark carried on as prosecutor in the O. J. Simpson case despite the tests that showed the jury did not like her one bit, with well-known results. Sometimes you must simply find a front. The conspirators in Shakespeare's *Julius Caesar* considered enlisting the respected Cicero to their cause, "for his silver hairs will purchase us a good opinion and buy men's voices to commend our deeds." And even if you can't get Cicero, you can invoke his name, or associate your position with a respected individual or group—the celebrity endorsement strategy of persuasion.

In 1939, when exiled European scientists living in America feared that the Nazis might be building an atomic bomb, they knew that they had little chance to reach and alert the height of the WASP establishment, so they enlisted the most famous ethnic alien of all, Albert Einstein, to write a letter to warn President Roosevelt of the danger. Still, even Einstein's credibility and celebrity were not enough. It took an old friend and advisor to the president, Alexander Sachs, to make the final presentation. Einstein's letter remained in a folder as Sachs warmed up Roosevelt with a story of how Napoleon had once received a proposal from an American who claimed he could build ships that could "move without sails" and attack England in any weather. Napoleon had the man thrown out for wasting his time. The man, Sachs explained, was Robert Fulton.

Sachs then emphasized the medical and power-generating potential of atomic fission, leaving the atomic bomb for last. Pitching the positive before describing the destructive aspects made atomic energy more consistent with America's and Roosevelt's values, but still made it clear that the Nazis could use atomic power to "blow us up" if we didn't get it first. Roosevelt got the message. As Sachs later said, "No scientist could sell it to him." Find someone they like, find someone like them.

Attitude Adjustment — Make Them Dislike the Opposition

If you don't go to the top dog, your opposition might. Like many boat-rockers, Galileo made enemies. When he published his *Dialogue on the Two Chief World Systems*, it was hugely popular—cleverly written and clearly presenting the heliocentric case. The success of the book was the first strike against Galileo. The second was the book's timing. The Pope's authority was under attack by the Protestant Reformation and he couldn't tolerate any more earthshakers. Galileo's enemies exploited the situation by suggesting to the Pope that the character Simplicio, the blockheaded champion of geocentricism in the *Dialogue*, was a personal jab at his holiness. They even suggested that the book's publisher's colophon, three fishes, was actually intended to poke fun at the Pope's three recently promoted nephews. This attack on Galileo (implying that he was making a personal, ad hominem attack on the Pope) helped to provoke the Pope's threatening, *ad baculum* ("Care to try our new rack, Mr. Smartypants?") response. Galileo had the facts of the universe on his side, but little good it did him.

Does ill-disposing an audience toward an opponent have any real bearing on the legitimacy of your main argument? Perhaps not, but it is still one of Aristotle's rules of rhetoric. How you use it depends upon the rules of the house you're playing in. The audience will punish you if they think you are cruel, unfair, or dishonest to your opponent, but from innuendo to blatant calumny, from name-calling to questioning motives, it never stops. I invest a lot of time listening to recordings of academic lectures, and even the most respected professors regularly use funny, demeaning voices when they quote the positions

of the opposition. Thomas Jefferson wrote that "resort is had to ridicule only when reason is against us." But Jefferson was probably just frustrated because he was too well brought up to indulge in the art, one in which Mark Twain excelled. Twain's self-deprecating ridicule deflated many an absurd proposition, as in this characterization of the anthropocentric argument:

> Man has been here 32,000 years. That it took a hundred million years to prepare the world for him is proof that that is what it was done for. I suppose it is, I dunno. If the Eiffel Tower were now representing the world's age, the skin of paint on the pinnacle-knob at its summit would represent man's share of that age; and anybody would perceive that that skin was what the tower was built for. I reckon they would, I dunno.

The cleverness and clarity of the vivid analogy make it a powerful "straw man" characterization of another's argument. Unfair—but entertaining, effective, and persuasive.

The wine of persuasion is pressed from the grapes of three vines. So far we have been dealing with what Aristotle called pathos—appealing to feelings, putting the audience in a good mood, or evoking their fear to motivate them. The pathos of persuasive communication is intertwined with two other vines, ethos and logos. Ethos is the credibility of the source, and logos the logic of the argument. Trying to separate the three does them damage, since "getting" a logical argument can be as pleasing to your brain chemistry as helping an agreeable person. I will separate them gently.

Credibility

Credentials are but one side of credibility. The sign may say "Fresh," but the fish still has to pass the smell test. Smell, probably our most primal sense, tells us when to start whipping that flagella

to escape a toxic part of the swamp. Sometimes we "smell" with our eyes and ears. By this I mean all the nonverbal cues, tone, gesture, eye contact, that tell us whether to trust someone. The classic example is the 1960 Kennedy–Nixon presidential debate. The perceived winner of the debate famously depends upon whether you saw the debate on television or heard it on radio. Those who watched it on television believed that Kennedy won, but radio listeners who could not see the faces of the two men thought that Nixon won. On radio, Nixon sounded fine, but on television he looked sweaty, sallow, shifty-eyed, unshaven. Between Nixon and the handsome, composed, tanned Kennedy, the choice was obvious.

One cruel but effective anti-Nixon advertisement consisted of a picture of his face and the words "Would you buy a used car from this man?" As Nixon learned, but never mastered, in order to be believed you have to look like a truth-teller. Your body communicates persuasiveness if you face your audience directly with a forward and open posture and build eye contact at a comfortable rate. You have to trust yourself, be yourself, but always look like a winner, no matter how you think things are going, because what is your alternative? Who will side with someone who smells like a loser?

Humans are also innately fine-tuned to detect cheaters—otherwise, selfless human behavior might never have evolved. Altruism in humans is hard to explain, unless we take into account the expectation of reciprocation. I would be more likely to share my gazelle meat with the rest of the tribe if I can expect similar treatment later on. Individuals who cheat when it comes their turn to share can obviously prosper—unless they are held in check by the cheater detectors in other tribe members that coevolved with altruism.

Humans make decisions based more on their cheater detection system than on logic. Your audience will partially judge your credibility—the power they grant you to influence their decision making—on your degree of interest in the outcome. If you will clearly benefit, if they know you are working on commission, fair enough, they see what's in it for you; now what's in it for them? But if they suspect that you have a plan to gain in excess of fair exchange, credibility drops. A neutral party with nothing to gain is more credible, and a person who knowingly acts against their own interest is most trustworthy of all. This last state is one that is often faked. "I'll get in trouble with my sales manager for telling you this, but we have an even better deal for you on . . ." Logically, we know that the car salesman will not act against his own self-interest, but he is trying to disarm our cheater detector, not to appeal to our logical calculations.

Persuasive language is also the language of immediacy. Franklin Roosevelt, in a "fireside chat" radio address explaining the rubber shortage during World War II, did not make a generalized statement like "The unknown factor is the amount of unused rubber held in private stocks." Instead he personalized it in terms of "We don't know how much unused rubber is stored in *your* basement, in *your* barn." Roosevelt knew the medium and used it brilliantly. The result was mountains of surplus rubber donated by millions of people who felt he was speaking directly with them, his energetic voice projecting confidence and credibility.

The sound of persuasive truth comes briskly with expression and animation. Hesitant or slow speech with many disruptions and incomplete sentences communicates exactly the opposite: fear and

incompetence. Both an overly soft and an overly loud voice communicate insecurity. Notice the location of "uh"s and "uhm"s in speech. They often follow an exaggeration or impolite characterization. They are not just irritating filler, but a cue that even the speaker knows that they have gone too far.

If, however, you overdo any of the positive attributes, you also risk activating your audience's defenses. Stand too close, make too much eye contact at first, speak too energetically in their face, and your audience may feel pressured or distracted by your overbearing manner. Any sign of pressuring is a cue to people that they are being forced into inconsistency. In response, they begin mounting resistance.

Convincing liars, experts at not triggering your resistance, have many of the skills that make successful leaders. They control not only their face with a relaxed smile, forward lean, and eye contact; they also control the self-manipulation (ring fiddling, face touching) and vocal tension that tip the hand of the less skillful. Transparent liars tend to gesture with less energy and enthusiasm and to speak more slowly, less fluently, and in a higher pitch. Unfortunately, those who tell the truth in this way are often perceived to be lying.

It may be as bad to be a poor truth-teller as it is to be a good liar. From the gallows perspective of the disbelieved, it is the same to be hanged as a fool or as a knave. Persuasive presentations have a bit of tension to them, and tension will make your voice higher, so you can start working days ahead to lower your voice with this exercise. Repeatedly vocalize extended "uhhhh"s and "ahhhh"s in lower and lower voices. Begin this practice weeks before a presentation, or better, make this a part of your daily routine. Sound like a confident alpha primate and you can lead the pack.

Appropriate visual display also inspires confidence. Would you attempt persuasive communication with your hands over your face? Wouldn't that imply that you have something to hide? Then why would you make the majority of a presentation standing in the dark beside a projection screen, revealing only the data on your slides? If they wanted just the data you could give it to them in print instead of dragging their bodies down to a meeting. Getting some light on your face means you are willing to be judged for trustworthiness. Your intelligence and empathy come through as you respond quickly and accurately to the changing audience response. If it is a meeting, they need to see you in order to trust you.

A skilled and dynamic presenter is perceived as more trustworthy, and if the importance of the persuasive presentation merits it, and you have the time to do so, your best presentation will come from writing the whole thing out, perfecting it, studying it, practicing it, but then never looking at the written text during the presentation. Bring notes, write down your quotes, know your opening and closing cold, follow your outline—but don't read. During the presentation this extensive preparation will help you relax and respond to the audience.

This practice and preparation will not make you "too slick." Being perceived as too slick is simply another result of being unskilled or inattentive—usually resulting in underestimating the sensitivity and intelligence of your audience. As Mark Twain advised, the best presentation has "been carefully prepared in private and tried on a plaster cast, or an empty chair, or any other appreciative object that will keep quiet until the speaker has got his matter and his delivery limbered up so that they will seem impromptu to the audience." You will have the chance to refine the language, hone the argument,

practice and learn it—but not memorize it. Think of it this way: You don't want a pilot who has *memorized* how to fly the plane, you want a pilot who has thoroughly *learned* how to fly the plane.

One who has evidence of experience and expertise should logically be more trusted. Most of us try to enhance our credibility by having our credentials trotted out during an introduction. If we have undertaken special research, studies, or travel, or devoted long experience to a topic, we will modestly let this be known. Perceived scarcity of expertise, for example testimony from the "world's foremost authority," or tests on "a machine borrowed from the CIA," can make it seem more important and (often unduly) credible. A celebrity with no expertise in the topic can have the same appeal of perceived scarcity and positive associations. But again, this strength when overdone can become a weakness. If your expertise places too great a distance between the audience's level of comprehension and your own, you can be perceived as arrogant, out of touch, or socially distant, not "one of us"—a possible cheater.

None of these concerns about appearance and articulation are true credibility, true ethos; they simply influence the perception of credibility, and perception equals reality.

Making a Rational Appeal

Now to logos. If flattering your audience and slamming your opponent don't do the job, you may actually have to present a rational argument. Just as for sports and games, societies have agreed upon the rules for objective argument based on standards and evidence, with rules for formal as well as for informal engagements. At times the rules may call for Logic with a capital L, but even that is just an agreement on how to play decision-making games. Logic bears the same relationship to most persuasion as the game of Go Fish does to the siege of Stalingrad.

Logical appeals have persuasive values beyond logic. Even if you are not using formal argumentation, there are some audiences

If the law is on your side, argue the law.
If the facts are on your side, argue the facts.
If neither are on your side, pound the table.

where simply using the *language* of formal debate signals that you share a similar background with them. You validate their experience, you are one of them, they will like you, you will be more persuasive. Logic also has an aesthetic quality to it. Following a path of reason, succeeding at a cognitive task, generates pleasure. Getting a logical argument is as pleasurable as getting a joke. An illogical path is displeasing, but you show them a better one, a pleasingly logical one, and they are happy again. You reveal problems and then lead to the solution. A basic rational appeal unfolds as follows:

- State your premise. Here's the problem and what they need to do about it.

- Follow with supporting evidence and, if necessary, support your evidence with warrants—subarguments that strengthen the connection of the evidence to the premise.

- To strengthen your position when there are concerns or opposition, you might concede some of your weak points and preemptively rebut attacks on others.

- Finally, restate your main argument and close with a memorable, emotionally powerful agent.

Before a sympathetic audience or when the other side will not have a voice, you usually will present just your side of an argument. But with an unsympathetic audience, or when an opponent will follow you, you should consider presenting both sides of the issue. If they are going to hear both sides anyway, your version of it, coupled with the arguments against it, can inoculate your audience against the position of the other side. This is what Twain did in his presentation of the "age of the earth—age of man" argument earlier. Consider inoculation when there are obvious weaknesses in your proposition. Better they hear it from you, along with your defense, than from anyone else.

Just as there are often two sides in a logical argument, there are two directions: from specific to general and from general to specific. To remember which form of argument is the inductive and which is the deductive, think of the big, general idea as a box. In *inductive* arguments you put specifics *into* the box to imply a general conclusion. This is a good pattern for a hostile audience where the smaller points of agreement build up to make the climactic conclusion inevitable. For example:

It's as hard as a rock,
    the feathers are glued on,
        its feet are nailed to the perch

—*this* is a dead parrot.

For *deductive* arguments, you *deduct* specifics from the big idea or premise and place them before the audience. These specifics il-

lustrate and demonstrate the truth you propose. A valid deductive argument also *descends* from the major premise through a minor premise to the conclusion. For example:

Successful practice justifies confidence.
    You have been practicing successfully for weeks.

        Your confidence is justified.

If the first two steps are true, then the conclusion must be true. Still, there are circumstances where the steps may be true by themselves, but the conclusion is false. For example: Dead parrots don't talk. This parrot doesn't talk. *This* is a dead parrot. It may be true, but it is not logically proven. The parrot just might not feel like talking. Also, true conclusions may be reached by means of faulty logic—the parrot just might happen to be dead. (We'll meet many of these species of faulty logic in the field guide that concludes this chapter.)

These simple inductive and deductive arguments are also the building blocks for complex persuasive efforts:

Cause/effect and *effect/cause* patterns combine inductive and deductive arguments to demonstrate a causal relationship between events.

Process of elimination patterns use a reductive line of reasoning, where you consider and eliminate a string of possible answers, except for the final one—the one you are proposing. As Sherlock Holmes said: "When you have eliminated the impossible, whatever remains, however improbable, must be the truth." The impossible options will have been previously eliminated by inductive and deductive arguments.

Problem-solving patterns lead the audience to define the problem and help shape a solution. The problem-solving inductive approach is particularly useful with a hostile audience. Ask for input, ideas to solve the problem, and compile them into a report on the ubiquitous white board or flip chart. (Some persuaders in group environments will employ only the appearance of participation, with the solution a foregone conclusion. This method is known as *interactive totalitarianism.*)

Argument by analogy applies your reasoning to an entirely different case. Twain was arguing by analogy with his Eiffel Tower model. Analogy may be persuasive—as when Franklin Roosevelt compared the "lend-lease" of old destroyers to Great Britain with lending a neighbor a garden hose when their house is on fire—but analogy is still not evidence.

The problem-solving approach works well with hostile audiences.

Evidence

Concrete, direct evidence is the strongest support for your claim. Galileo had the evidence of the telescope revealing the moons of Jupiter and the phases of Venus. His opponents cited the evidence of their naked eyes and "common sense." If the earth was moving, why didn't the shaking cause buildings to topple? Galileo's evidence required new technology and complex reasoning. To understand his argument, you had to understand the implications of the observations—just what does the observation that Venus has phases like the moon mean? Why is it relevant to the behavior of the earth?

Old ideas fight a fierce rearguard defense during which combatants will even overrule their own intellect. They will look through Galileo's telescope and see the phases of Venus and the moons around it, and yet claim this must be dust in the tube. They will deny evidence and their own intelligence to satisfy other needs. Intelligence is just a tool. Rationality is just an agreement. Ethical behavior is just a choice.

With evidence, your argument becomes more than just an assertion.

Evidence can be faked. While claiming that his telescope was a trick device Galileo's enemies planted forged documents in the Vatican archives to incriminate him. These were not the ignorant that were against him. These were the smartest people of the time, at the top of the power elite. They could easily have understood and seen the truth of the Copernican system, but they chose not to, because they stood to lose more than they would gain. People will reject the most concrete evidence if it points against their hopes and desires. As Machiavelli warned us in *The Prince:*

> Nothing is more difficult, more dangerous, or more doubtful in its success, than to lead in the introduction of change. For the innovator will have for his enemies all those who are well off under the existing order of things, and only lukewarm supporters in

those who might be better off under the new. This lukewarm support arises partly from the fear of adversaries who have the laws on their side, and partly from the incredulity of mankind, who will never admit the merit of anything new, until they have seen it in action. The result is that whenever the enemies of change make an attack, they do so zealously, while the others defend themselves so feebly as to endanger both themselves and their cause.

In spite of this, Machiavelli did leave a hopeful opening in his words "until they have seen it in action." Evidence such as a video or demonstration that shows your proposition in action is your best persuader. If you can create a simulation, a demonstration, a manifestation of your proposed order of things, do it. Tests of evidence include relevancy, materiality, clarity, and credibility, but the ultimate test is whether you can manifest it so your audience can see it for themselves.

Emotional/Motivational Appeals

If you hope to convince someone to adopt a new belief, you might try to hook them with an introduction that begins where they are and tweaks them. If you know that your audience advocates social justice, begin by showing evidence of social injustice. To convince potential customers of the value of a product, start with images of other people enjoying it and then demonstrate how it works. If you can get an endorsement from a respected authority, use it. Begin with vivid anecdotal evidence that supports your claim. "John made $55,000 in just three hours using our no-cash . . ." Or use selected numbers. "You own timberland, and within a decade the demand for timber will increase 150 percent yet the land allotted to timber will decline by 40 percent." The emotional hook makes the audience aware of the problem, open for the solutions that follow.

165

The sea of consumer junk around us is testimony to the power of this motivated sequence, a problem-solution pattern described by A. H. Monroe in the thirties. This is where the "sell benefits not features" maxim and the "what's in it for me?" standard come from. These five steps are the basic formula for persuasive advertisement.

ATTENTION STEP	Stop! Look! Listen!	*Dad falls in pain!*
NEED STEP	Show the problem and why it's important.	*He's having a heart attack! You have only seconds to act!*
SATISFACTION STEP	Show the solution and why it would work. Show them how the benefit exceeds the cost.	*Aspirin can help prevent heart damage during an attack.*
VISUALIZATION STEP	Get them to imagine the solution in action, experiencing the benefits in their minds.	*Aspirin on hand will give you the power to save your dad's life.*
ACTION STEP	Make it real, ask for the order.	*Buy aspirin now, before it's too late!*

The Power of Story

When smoothed out, this motivated sequence pattern becomes a little drama, a story of loss and redemption. Whatever the facts of your message, you can use them to paint such a vivid picture that the audience sees themselves in it. Tell the story in the present tense, second person, so that to the listeners, it is happening now, to them. Trial lawyers often use this technique of putting the jury in the place of their client. "You're waiting for the light to change,

thinking how much fun it will be to play with your children when you get home. Suddenly, you can feel the shock of bones breaking and nerves snapping as your head is thrown back at sixty-three miles an hour."

Influential people tell influential stories that resonate, that ring true to both the head and the heart. Thomas Jefferson was the classic passionate intellectual, and an accident in Paris gave him pause to express his character in a romantic verse to his lady-love, Maria Cosway. Leaping over a wall (to retrieve Maria's scarf, the story goes), he landed badly and broke his right wrist. This forced him to write with his left hand, the hand controlled by his right brain. One of the results of his "writing on the right side of the brain" was a 4,000 word love letter containing his famous "Dialogue between my head and my heart." In it, Jefferson's heart tells his head to "fill papers as you please with triangles & squares," but to stay out of important decision making. In the following excerpt, Jefferson's heart claims that his head has often misled him:

> . . . when the poor wearied souldier whom we over-took at Chickahomony with his pack on his back, begged us to let him get up behind our chariot, you [head] began to calculate that the road was full of souldiers, & that if all should be taken up our horses would fail in their journey. We drove on therefore. But soon becoming sensible you had made me do wrong, that tho we cannot relieve all the distressed we should relieve as many as we can, I turned about to take up the souldier; but he had entered a bye path, & was no more to be found; & from that moment to this I could never find him out to ask his forgiveness. . . . In short, my friend, as far as my recollection serves me, I do not know that I ever did a good thing on your suggestion, or a dirty one without it. I do for-ever then disclaim your interference in my province.

Jefferson's heart goes on to say that if the American patriots had made a rational calculation, they would never have taken on the superior wealth and military strength of the British Empire.

Jefferson's "dialogue" was a love letter written to a married lady, not so much to persuade her of anything, but to ease and occupy Jefferson's own mind during his recovery. ("A mind always employed is always happy. This is the true secret, the grand recipe for felicity.") His heart simply makes an inductive argument against following the judgment of his head, but I cite it here as an example of how appealing and persuasive a story can be. Imagine that you are in a persuasive situation where logic is against you. You acknowledge this, but then tell the story of Jefferson and the "poor wearied souldier" and his regret in not listening to his heart, and how it was heart (said Jefferson) that won us our independence. What logical argument could stand against the appeals to authority (Jefferson), to patriotism (America itself), and pity (the "poor wearied souldier")? So do like Jefferson said: Listen to your heart and convict this man, buy this car, marry me—in spite of your rational concerns.

(The persuasiveness of this argument cashes in upon favorable associations with Thomas Jefferson. If your audience's mental associations surrounding Jefferson involve good things—creative courage and intellectual leadership—it might do the trick. If, however, your audience associates Jefferson with bad things—racism and hypocrisy—it might well backfire.)

When trying to be persuasive, by definition you are trying to bring people to a given conclusion. Although, as Pascal observed, "we are better persuaded the reasons we discover ourselves than by those given to us by others," if you want people to reach a desired conclusion, state your conclusion explicitly. Remember the story of the blind men and the elephant. They all drew different conclusions about the nature of the whole elephant depending upon which piece of anatomical evidence they were examining with their hands. Even the same evidence can lead people to different conclusions. In informative communication, the point is to stimulate, to expand. In persuasion, the object is to narrow choices. If you want convergent thinking, define the point of convergence. You won't lose anyone who has been following your argument all along, and the explicit conclusion will direct the interpretation of the evidence among the more impressionable. In a persuasive effort, it's often risky to leave the conclusion open to interpretation.

Even when you successfully persuade your audience emotionally, you still need to give them the rational tools to support the belief. Paradoxically, the greater the emotional basis for the opinion, the more it must be masked by the appearance of logic. Your audience wants rational consistency with their individual subjective sets of values, attitudes, and beliefs. Even the "I hate 'em, let's kill 'em all" type of genocide pathology needs the "rational" fig leaf justification of some legendary offense from 600 years in the past. Feeling is a parade of elephants, and rationalization must follow after with a dustpan.

End with an Emotionally Charged Agent

Martin Luther King, Jr.'s great "I Have a Dream" speech was filled with stirring quotations and slogans, and ended with his dramatic vision of the future. It is so often cited, you probably know it by heart. This is your closing shot, your sit-down statement, your battle cry that remains in your audience's memory and continues to work for you after you have finished. It is the most important of all moments, but it should not stand alone, appearing out of nowhere. It should be a powerful reprise of a theme that you established at the beginning and have woven throughout your argument.

Present your theme and every important statement in the positive form. Say "Hold on tight!" instead of "Don't let go!" Say "If the glove don't fit, you must acquit!" rather than a negative form like "If the glove constricts, no one convicts."

It's a bumper sticker. This theme or slogan must be simple, visual, understandable, and make the audience smugly confident. It must give them what they need to act as you desire. If they need courage, the last statement must give them courage. If they need a moral position, a vision of the future, or even a rational fact, give it to them and let it work. The "glove don't fit" couplet was a smug mantra in the pocket of every member of O. J.'s jury to give them comfort after their decision. If questioned on the street about their verdict, they could pull it out and use it in their own defense.

The triplet is another powerful tool of demagoguery. The Nazis had the people chanting "Ein volk, ein reich, ein führer!" In the closing arguments of the O. J. case, O. J.'s defense lawyer had a triplet ready, one that he had been using since the beginning of the trial. "My client could not, would not, and did not commit these crimes." The prosecutor also had a triplet, "He did it. He did it. He did it." But that was just lame repetition without variation. The defense had the winning triplet—aesthetically superior use of theme and variation. Fun to remember, fun to repeat.

Aristotle said that "simplicity makes the uneducated more effective than the educated when addressing popular audiences." But that sells simplicity short. You can be educated as hell and still have the common touch, the skill and determination to reach to the child in each of us with something simple, understandable, and comforting. A clear direction in a chaotic world. That is the difference between informing and persuading; informing tells people what is in the past, present, or future but persuasion shows us what could be and directs us toward it.

And So — in Conclusion . . .

- Understand and appeal to your audience's preexisting values, attitudes, and beliefs.
- State your proposition, establishing a theme that carries the idea throughout.
- Combine rational and emotional appeals to your best advantage for a given audience. Aim for the highest common denominator of feeling and thinking for every audience.
- Make people like you and believe in you by complimenting them and emphasizing your similarities.
- Use concrete evidence or that which looks like concrete evidence.
- Push your strong points and minimize your weak ones, including any opposition.
- End with a reprise of your proposition, a battle cry demanding action that keeps working for you after you are done. Such as:

Lord, let me always be a seeker after the truth.
And deliver me from those who think they have found it.

Logical Fallacies: A Brief Field Guide to Disengaging Intelligence

The first group of logical fallacies comes from Aristotle's advice to "make the audience well-disposed toward yourself and ill-disposed toward your opponent." If you have a choice about who will present your argument, make sure it is your best-liked person. Fortify your position with as many "mom and apple-pie" associations as possible. As for overtly putting down your opponent, assign that to a designated "attack dog." Remember that the cultural context determines the acceptability of these actions. In dramatic, literary, and psychological studies we learn to root down to true motivations, but in most other circumstances it is unacceptable to question an opponent's motivation.

Liking

"Be liked and you will never want . . . It's who you know and the smile on your face." So believed Willy Loman in the play *Death of a Salesman*. It's true, charisma beats logic any day. But when they stop liking you, you've got nothing.

Personal Attack
(ad hominem)

Using the race, sex, or character of the person as an argument. "What would a white male know about this anyway?" There are three subspecies, the abusive, the motive, and the *tu quoque* (you too). Never a legitimate argument, particularly when it is on target.

Prejudicial Labeling

Application of glowing/disparaging generalizations. "I'm the creative one, let me do it!" "Maybe I'm the only one here who cares about education, but . . ." and attorney Gerry Spence's characterizing a case as "corporate greed vs. human need."

In addition to making them like you and dislike your opponent, you can make your audience like themselves by giving them the responsibility to help the downtrodden. The appeal to pity gives the audience feelings of God-like power.

Appeal to Pity
(ad misericordiam)

 Begging for favor on the basis of need or effort. "Yes, their version is better, and they did it in two weeks, but we've been working on our version for over four years!"

Perhaps you don't actually have God on your side of the issue, but you can always make that claim, whether the god you invoke is unitary or multitudinous.

Appeal to Authority
(ad vericundiam)

Dropping the name of a revered authority as a supporter of the proposition. "But this is how they do it at Disney!" This is persuasive because opposition to the proposal may be construed as an attack on the revered authority. Also, note the *ad antiquitam* and *ad novitam* variants, using the appeal of the ancient or the modern respectively.

Appeal to the Crowd
(ad populum)

The bandwagon argument; using an alleged majority view as evidence that the proposition is correct. A mocking "Everybody knows that . . ." followed by laughter. Successful in larger audiences where it can harness mob instincts.

Although they are just as often applied individually, the next persuasive techniques also come in the classic "carrot and the stick" or the "good cop–bad cop" pairings.

Reciprocation

A small kindness obligates the recipient to further cooperation. "Wow! A cup of coffee! I *will* buy that Mercedes now!"

Appeal to Force
(ad baculum)

As Machiavelli advised, "It is far safer to be feared than loved." Coercing compliance with threats seldom requires an actual stick; just a "You don't have to agree with the game plan—unless you value your job."

Physical threats are not the only ways fear can be persuasive. The fly-by-night salesman of The Music Man *conned an entire town using the following techniques.*

False Scarcity

Forcing action by creating a false sense of urgency. "Today only! We have only a few remaining!"

Appeal Citing Adverse Consequences
(ad consequentiam)

Stating the unpleasant consequences of accepting or not accepting a logical proposition. "If we accept Galileo's argument, the Protestants will take it as a sign of weakness."

Slippery Slope

Also known as the thin end of the wedge or the camel's nose. "If we let a volunteer in, soon we'll all be out of work."

Storytelling has a special persuasiveness, because, as we saw earlier, it walks the same mental pathways as direct experience. The best story, seemingly related to the issue in question, may be entirely unrelated to rational decision making, but it may well be the most persuasive.

Confusing Analogy with Evidence

Gloria Steinem's "A woman needs a man like a fish needs a bicycle" is a brilliant analogy to make a pointed assertion, but it is not evidence to support a proposition.

Confusing Anecdote with Proof

"Backpacking is for idiots. Let me tell you about my experience with backpacking."

Just as you might work to ill-dispose your audience toward your opponent, you can also ill-dispose them to your opponent's story by mistelling it or by using trickery.

Straw Man

Misrepresentation of an opposing position through extension or exaggeration. "You think we should give everyone a free ride. You want to turn our company into some kind of hippie commune!"

Complex Question

The "have you stopped beating your dog" question. A hybrid of two unrelated points, one of which may make an invalid assumption. "Don't you believe in supporting the reorganization and better serving our customers?"

Non Sequitur

(non sequitur)

The conclusion does not necessarily follow. "If we are on the side of God, then God is on our side."

Invalid Disjunction

An "either-or" argument also known as the false dilemma. "We can either entertain or educate, but we can't do both!" Also: the *ad temperantiam* argument. The simple-minded assertion that the best answer lies at a midpoint between polar opposites.

As these fallacies take on the appearance of logic, they manage to pass unnoticed until expressed in the most outrageous forms.

Post Hoc Coincidence

(post hoc, ergo propter hoc)

Maintaining that an event that follows another in time was caused by the preceding one. Correlation without causation. "Women got the vote in the 1920s and the next thing you know the stock market crashed."

Circle Argument

Repetition of the same idea is not evidence. "Politicians are all cynics. Why? Because anyone who thinks cynically is a politician at heart."

Argument from Ignorance
(ad ignorantiam)
The proposition that something is true because it has not been proven false and vice versa. "We've tried to teach presentation skills for years. It can't be taught!"

Other strategies attempt to distract us from or distort the evidence to support one side of an issue.

Observational Selection
Basing claims on biased samples. Counting only the hits and ignoring the misses. "Ninety-seven percent of our customers rate us as excellent!" (What about the noncustomers?)

Confusing Similar with Same
"He looks like JFK, let's make him the leader." Or "The root of this plant looks like liver; I bet it would help your cirrhosis."

Fallacy of Composition
Confusing the parts with the whole. "Look at those beautiful feathers! That must be one delicious bird!" Conversely: the Fallacy of Division, confusing the whole with the parts.

Confusing Obscurity with Profundity
Style masquerading as substance or the emperor's new clothes. "She's brilliant, it was so deep, so . . . Oh, I just can't explain it!"

Hasty Generalization

Applying a judgment based on stereotypical expectations. "What do you expect from suburban kids?"

And you can always count on the other refuge of the scoundrel . . .

Special Pleading

"You don't understand! Just trust me, I know all about this."

. . . and of the dullard.

Repetition ad Nauseam

Repetition ad nauseam. Repetition ad nauseam.

I was tempted to close this bestiary of illogic with a high-minded condemnation of fallacies such as, "thus do cunning men pass for wise," but, in truth, most of us employ these fallacies every day. Using logical fallacies does not mean that your cause is unjust or untrue, but it does offer weak spots for opponents to attack. And when fallacies are used against you, naming them and challenging them is a fair defense.

Just be sure that a defense is called for. Correcting another's faulty logic is not the most endearing social act. You can seldom win someone over to your side by bludgeoning them with your erudition.

CHAPTER 8
DIRECT ACTION — PUTTING THE COGS IN COGNITION

A ction is the omega and the alpha. When we began this book, we considered communication to have five stages: getting attention, maintaining interest, informing, convincing, and finally, directing action—as if communication were a linear process leading to action only if you were trying to get a vote or make a sale. But, as you have seen, even to share knowledge, you must often convince others to take action and make discoveries for themselves. Thus, cycles of these five stages of communication turn as little wheels within the bigger wheels of individual growth. We are not just at the end with this chapter, then, we are also at the beginning.

This sequence of action and reaction bears a rough resemblance to the experiential learning cycle described by David Kolb in the 1970s. Kolb and others took this cycle further to describe individual styles of learning. Some of us prefer the action part, others the theory part, but for the cycle to complete, for growth to occur, you need to bring people through the entire cycle. If they are stuck in the theoretical mode, you need to encourage them into action.

Sometimes all you need is to get out of the way, just stand by and be a "midwife at the birth of understanding." As Stephen J. Gould put it, "People, as curious primates, dote on concrete objects that can be seen and fondled." They are probably going to want to try an action you offer, if you will only make it available and the directions clear enough. Others will derive pleasure from exploration and discovery just as you do.

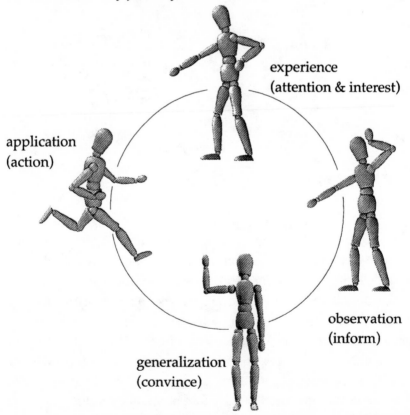

When you wrap the linear structure of a presentation into a cycle of experiential learning, bringing the audience to the action or application phase creates a new experience that begins the cycle again.

So now, moving molecules in the brain is no longer enough. Now we must have muscular action in the external world. We'll look at directing action from the authoritative, stimulus-response relationship through the constructive, mentoring relationship, first looking at a principle that will affect performance at every level.

L'Esprit de l'escalier

Imagine you're at a party and some jerk makes a clever comment at your expense. You're speechless, and only as you are leaving do you think of the world's greatest comeback. Why couldn't you access this brilliance at the right moment? The French term for this little bit of torment is *l'esprit de l'escalier* or staircase wit, so called because that's where you tend to be when the brain finally delivers—too late to do you any good.

The scientific term is the Yerkes-Dodson Law, which describes the inverted U-shaped response of performance through increasing degrees of arousal. Basically this law states that for a given task, you do your best work when you are not overly complacent and not overly worked up. We have seen this stated many times in other ways earlier in this book. Remember in Daloz's matrix (Chapter 1) that growth is fostered by a combination of high challenge and high support—another way of stating "Get them turned on but not freaked out."

But why "staircase" wit? Imagine your response when the reptile at the party delivers his barb. Your temporary inability to return instantly with a scorpion-sting retort may be because the insult has aroused you beyond the point of optimal performance. Or, you may have relaxed with the champagne and the late hour and have dropped into a suboptimal state for witty response. Later, however, on the staircase, the physical exertion and attention required to keep from falling will perk the somnolent or calm the enraged. You shift toward the optimal state, and the perfect response pops into your brain—too late to do you a bit of good. *L'esprit de l'escalier.*

There are countless other incidents where the U-shaped response curve serves you either well or ill. You need energy and presence when communicating with a group—you need arousal—but only to the extent that it helps you. Too much arousal becomes disruptive anxiety. In conversation and in presentations, there are optimal levels of arousal for optimal effect. Get too worked up and you can blow it—be too complacent and you will have no effect.

This goes for your audience as well. You want them to do things, to try things, and you want them to do them well. For both your sakes, for communication to occur you need to bring this factor under conscious control. The first control strategy is practice. Habituation—preexposure to the stressful circumstances—will reduce your arousal level to a more productive level. Habituation is combat training, not book learning. Whatever the task, it means getting it right

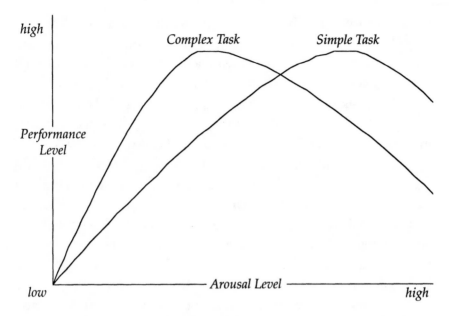

The Yerkes-Dodson Law states that performance increases with arousal level, peaks, and then begins to drop off.

in a realistic rehearsal. Benjamin Franklin wrote to a friend regarding the necessity of learning to swim by actually practicing, not by just reading and trying to remember the instructions when the need arises. Franklin warned that, upon accidentally falling in the water, ". . . till you have obtained this experimental confidence in the water, I cannot depend on your having the necessary presence of mind to recollect that posture and the directions I gave you relating to it. The surprise may put all out of your mind. For though we value ourselves on being reasonable creatures, reason and knowledge seem on such occasions to be of little use to us; and the brutes, to whom we allow scarce a glimmering of either, appear to have the advantage of us."

"Reason and knowledge" are of little use to us under high-stress circumstances, simply because we can't get to them. Rehearsal of the stressful circumstance, however, allows us to take it more calmly and to access judgment and conscious control while procedural memory takes care of the swimming. Franklin aside, here we have advantage over the "brutes." A deer caught in quicksand doesn't stop struggling and think to itself, "Relax, breathe deep, these humans with the ropes are just here to help me." You, however, about to face an audience, can say to yourself, "Of course I'm excited, I'm about to speak to an important group. I feel energized and ready to do a great job. I can visualize them responding with the same enthusiasm I feel myself." You have rational control. You can control your physiological state by consciously taking control of your breathing, or burning off some of that adrenaline by walking up a flight of stairs before the event. A primary skill of performance is the ability to quickly adjust your level of arousal to meet changing demands—and the demands must be changing or things get boring. Much of the art of coaching others seems to be helping others develop the skill to adjust their arousal level for optimum performance.

As an interactive communicator, you are also a coach, constantly asking your audience to do things: to role-play, to try on a new idea, to just share a new perspective. You take the lead in adjusting their arousal level for optimal performance. If the arousal level is too low, you can introduce competitive games that tap energy from that reptilian brain. A little bit of this kind of arousal enhances learning. But what about scary activities such as role-playing? If you are only going to do it once, you might decide to spring the exercise on the participants so that they do not have time to get worked up about it. But once you spring it on one group, the cat is out of the bag, and the others will start to fret. Loss of control is a surefire stress generator. If they are having too much trouble with the task, making too many errors, then they may be too worked up. The next time around, make a greater effort to reduce stress by telling them more explicitly up front what you will expect—better explaining the purpose of the activity, asking for volunteers, or conversing privately with potential participants before you ask them to take part.

On the other side of the curve, if you need people to be in a high state of arousal, it's going to be easier for them to find the appropriate level if, in practicing, they have gone beyond where they need to

be. The coach screaming at the team to "Get out there and rip their guts out, tear off their arms, break their legs, and shove that ball down their throats!" probably doesn't mean it. But even in performing a role onstage, at some time during rehearsal, the actor often learns by exceeding the character's arousal and then dropping back, rather than only working up from below.

The Yerkes-Dodson Law has an apparent contradiction with an earlier proposition in this book. Emotional stress, high arousal, and big excitement, like getting chased by the lion, not only help us to run away, but fix the event in our memory. So why is high arousal not good for all performance and all learning? Under high stress we revert to old patterns, we do things well that our ancient ancestors had to do well to survive. We can run and fight and vividly remember which cave not to venture into, and we just don't need those later-evolved parts of our brain to interfere. Moderate arousal helps us achieve "modern" complex tasks, but in high arousal, in threat situations, we revert to lower brain function and old habits. Under threat we dismiss intrinsic goals ("I want to grow as an artist") and look more to the external masters of reward and punishment ("Cripes! Run! It's going to eat us!").

Under threat we also become more susceptible to persuasion and modeling by others, and some people will take advantage of this to gain compliance by stressing you out with a sudden attack, or wearing you down with a constant bombardment of inputs so they can reshape you, never giving you time to think as you move away from higher brain function and become a herd animal, a lemming following the leader over the cliff, injecting more and more fear into your trip so you can't reason, there is no reason, you just do because you're overwhelmed and there goes everyone else.

Military basic training uses stress just to this purpose—to break down individualism and build the bond to the group and instant obedience to authority. Further training under simulated combat reduces the arousal generated by violent threats to one's being and ensures a reliable response under the chaotic conditions of combat—just like Ben Franklin's theory on learning to swim.

Sometimes small things, such as a few words of encouragement, can make the difference. One memorable guide led my group through the excavations of the Roman site in the English city of Bath. She built not only our understanding of the ancient site, but also our trust in her and in ourselves. She concluded our visit in the portal to the elegant Pump Room, where we could look in at the string quintet and the formally dressed waiters racing between a hundred white tablecloths. On the far side of the room was the fountain pouring out the sulfurous, allegedly curative, water that has drawn people for thousands of years. It was an intimidating spectacle for us modest American tourists.

We believed in our guide, though, and best of all, she showed how she believed in us with her parting words. "And now, if you wish, you can follow in the footsteps of Elizabeth the first, Samuel Johnson, and Jane Austen and walk on past all those snooty waiters and help yourself to a drink of the nasty stuff." She gave us the power and the challenge and the vision to make the final journey as

well as if she had said, "Trust the force, Luke." Had she not been there, had she not given us her words of encouragement, I doubt we would have risked it. But now and forever more, I can stride with confidence across the Pump Room in Bath, past all the snooty waiters, and help myself to a drink of the nasty stuff.

Our guide led us to the water, and made it easier for us to drink. She reduced our anxiety and our reluctance to take action by changing our thoughts and feelings, telling us that we had the right to drink from the fountain and that the waiters and the waters were not as superior as we felt.

Although crossing a room and getting a drink of water is a pretty simple task, the psychology of the whole event, if broken down minutely, could become quite complex. So let's begin with an even simpler, if more critical task, from the battlefield—the order given at the battle of Bunker Hill, "Don't fire until you see the whites of their eyes." This is a very simple behavior command: When you see this, do this. Stimulus–response is the lowest level of task complexity in

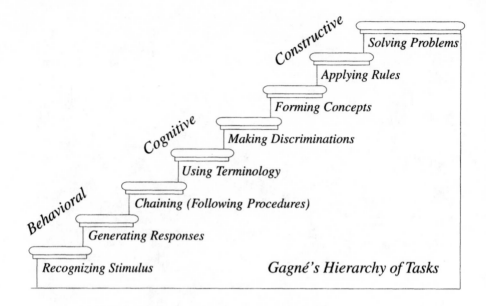

Gagné's Hierarchy of Tasks

a hierarchy proposed by psychologist Robert M. Gagné. We will use a modification of his hierarchy to climb to the creative level that we aspire to in the end. The lower steps are simple, stimulus-response, tasks. Midway up, we move into cognitive, thought-requiring tasks, and we'll end at the creative peak.

Stimulus-Response

If you want a response from someone, make sure that they recognize the stimulus. State your command specifically, precisely, and in a positive form. If you can come up with a vivid, fresh, and catchy phrase that says it all, then put on your general's hat and best uniform so you will look as if you have the power of reward and punishment and repeat it up and down the lines. If your directive slogan takes on a life of its own, it becomes much stronger than any rational argument. "Don't fire until you see the whites of their eyes" is not a positive form of the command, but it is clear enough.

Repeating precisely the same message builds precision in the response—"tab A into slot B" behavior. Once you decide on a desired action, clarity and precision make achievement more probable.

If your action agreement involves a measurable factor, such as conserving water, stating a defined (and achievable) goal such as 15 percent reduces potential frustration. Define the target and people are far more likely to hit it. If you want action as the result of a formal presentation, come to a conclusion that is a clear call for action; present a challenge, offer a plan, or make an appeal for help.

If your suggestion for action has no competition, then it will continue to dominate until a better one comes along. Totalitarian regimes work first to control communications media to eliminate competition. Conversely, advertising has become desperately creative because of the pressure of competing suggestions from other advertisers. How do you get your directive to punch through the noise? The uncreative settle for repetition.

Sheer repetition will bore a message into the subconscious until it reaches a critical mass and enters into your long-term memory. These are usually action commands that will guide your behavior in uncertain times: "Insist on Acme Rocket Shoes!" More subtle manipulators will also try to embed action commands within other messages. The concealed command gets punched just enough to drive it into the subconscious but not enough to make it apparent to the conscious mind. Consider two examples with the same conscious message:

> "I know it's tough to **pay attention** this late in the day."
> "I know it's late, but I don't want you to **fall asleep**."

These two embedded commands will produce very different actions without the listeners becoming aware of it. The champion trickster, Brer Rabbit, implanted the idea that led to his escape from Brer Fox by repeatedly begging "Please don't throw me in that briar patch." These artful suggestions led his listener to the desired action by making him think that it was his own idea. Benjamin Franklin also considered himself a benign yet artful trickster, relating with pride his success in founding fire departments, police departments, philosophical societies, and even universities by keeping his involvement in the background. He developed a strategy of bringing up ideas at club meetings as "something he had heard" and asking others what they thought. He left ideas lying about like lost wallets and allowed others to pick them up and lay claim to them.

The lowest roads in persuasion and behavior control attempt to change beliefs without offering explanation. Like Pavlov's dog who drools when he hears the bell, people respond automatically and unconsciously to certain stimuli. Used manipulatively in generating action, salespeople will ask a series of questions that will get you in the habit of saying "yes," rewarding these yes responses with positive feedback so that when you get to the time for agreement you are far more likely to continue with another yes. If in speaking before a group of home owners you know that your final objective is a positive vote to build a lake, you might start right away by asking for a show of hands of everyone who enjoys nature and wildlife and then compliment them for their stewardship of the planet. After a little while, ask for a show of hands on all who would like to see the value of their property grow, and then compliment them on their financial savvy. Build to the climactic moment when you ask for the show-of-hands vote on the lake. The best predictor of someone's future action is their past action. Shape the present and you control the future. Perfect attendance gets you a gold star. Pecking at the wrong button gets you an electric shock. The immediate, extrinsic consequences of your actions shape your future behavior.

We often manipulate our audience's behavior in ways we do not intend. Throughout any interaction, you naturally tend to reward the responses you want to encourage and punish or ignore the ones you don't want. If you repeatedly punish "wrong" answers by humiliating the respondents in a guessing game for which you have all the right answers, no one will want to respond.

So if you want to communicate adult to adult, don't stimulate a childish response. If you begin a training session for adults with "Good morning! Ohhh, that wasn't very good! Let's try again . . . Gooood mooorning!" you may well activate the behavior patterns

that served your audience best when they were in the second grade. Forcing the group to repeat the greeting until it satisfies your standards is basic operant conditioning, changing their actions through external rewards and punishments.

Chaining — Making Procedures Easier

Chaining, the next level, links simple stimulus-response tasks into sequences that must be followed in proper order, such as "Stop, drop, and roll" if you catch on fire. You stop first, then you drop.

You can make a behavioral chain, a desired procedure, easier for your audience to follow by giving them tools to help them access the proper sequence, such as a checklist or memory aid like a rhyme. Try to take advantage of tools that they already have. They may never have done the whole thing, but if they have already mastered most of the parts, the whole will be a lot easier.

If you want people to attend a meeting, come to your yard sale, or show up to vote, make it easy for them—include a map showing them where to go. If a battery has to go in a certain way, design a device that precludes error. If you want a desired action, narrow the possible choices with "forcing functions"; design constraints that make them select the right one in the right sequence.

Forcing functions and design constraints have an oppressive sound to them, but when they eliminate the bad work, they are liberating. As an information architect, you're getting paid to calculate the neural load—the cognitive, emotional, and physical burden you are laying on folks—and to relentlessly chop away any deadweight.

Tasks have dimensions as well as weight. A narrow and shallow task requires few choices and short sequences to complete. It is a short, single chain. A room with a single light switch on the wall makes the task of turning on the lights narrow and shallow—as it should be. A bank of many unlabeled switches makes the task of getting the lights on unnecessarily wider. Unnecessary width to a task generates anomie, the flavor of frustration experienced when you can't be sure what to do. Unnecessary depth generates further alienation—you have to jump through so many hoops that you have little energy left for meaningful tasks. Having to go call the custodian to come in on his day off and unlock the control panel just to flip a switch makes lighting the room unnecessarily deeper.

Such basic stuff should follow simple, conventional rules: accelerator pedal on the right, brake pedal on the left. When an audience activity, such as filling out a response card, requires onetime special instructions, then they should be right there, available to short-term memory for them to use and discard. It should not require them to consume the time and energy to put it into long-term memory. The object is to engage intelligence to expand consciousness, not to wear it down with petty, peevish, perverse little frustrations. Make mundane tasks clear and simple, narrow and shallow, so your audience's energy can go to meaningful tasks.

Cognitive Tasks — Thinking Required

Conversely, meaningful activities that are wide and deep enrich our lives. Meaningful activities that generate pleasure with their undertaking need this greater width and depth to engage and reward curiosity and intelligence. Vacations characteristically broaden the

options with a wide variety of activities; your reward is freedom from both frustration and alienation. Hobbies reward with depth, allowing you to pursue the activity to deeper and deeper sequences. Few scholars can match the depth of knowledge reached by the relentless burrowing of an intrinsically motivated hobbyist.

Learning the shared names, making distinctions between similar items, making inferences based on partial data, knowing rules and applying them are all parts of intelligent behavior. In the historical novel *The Sand Pebbles*, Holman, the engineer-protagonist, dismisses Po-han, his Chinese engine room assistant, as an ignorant "monkey see–monkey do" coolie. The author described the stimulus-response relationship: "Po-han knew what to do, but he did not know what it was that he did . . . when he twisted a valve he did not realize that he was opening or closing it. To Po-han, all that he did was isolated little magics that moved a pressure gauge pointer or a water level back to the right place." In a great scene of the book, Holman sets out to teach Po-han the terminology, rules, and concepts that would enable him to grasp "the big magic that would make a living whole out of all the little magics." Holman becomes a mentor, giving his Po-han the tools to build his own understanding.

Naming Names

In earlier times, intelligence, education, and wisdom were all seen as functions of memorization. The more varied the language, situations, stories, examples, rules, and terminology we could draw upon to guide our actions in a given situation, the smarter we were. It works in a pinch.

Sometimes the names are not important to the action. In changing individual behavior, the name "Yerkes-Dodson Law" is unimportant. Knowing this name is certainly no substitute for understand-

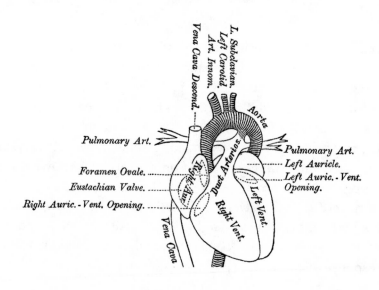

ing and applying the principle, but knowing the name will help anyone pursue the issue further through research and discussion. Learning the terminology helps you to do your work.

If you want your audience to be able to make symbolic representations and engage in discussion, they need to learn the names of things. Putting the thingy in the whatsits before you do that funny motion with it is not going to lead very far. Remembering new terminology is basically a function of rehearsal either through contextual association or through tricks of mnemonics. (Remember: Inductive logic puts specifics into a box of general truth, deductive logic takes specifics out.) If learning the names of things is an important part of the desired task, then help your audience with any tools you know or can develop with the aid of suggestions from the audience.

Discrimination

Distinguishing between similar items is another subtask that you can help your audience to do better. If you want someone to separate the wheat from the chaff, you could just teach the procedure of winnowing. But without the ability to distinguish when the task is sufficiently done, they would never know when to stop. If discrimination is an important skill for your audience to develop, you should hone these skills by using lots of examples, constantly increasing the fineness of the distinctions.

Again, watch intrinsically motivated hobbyists displaying their skills at discrimination. They love nothing better than gathering before the objects of their desire and playing games of identifying more and more precise distinctions. This skill practice, along with sharing definitions of the fine points and coupled with articulations of more and more precise terminology, is a basic social pleasure. When the consequences of error can be serious, such as in mushroom hunting or heart surgery, sharpening discrimination between similar items is quite useful.

Concept Forming

Concepts have to be assembled from partial cues, and are highly variable. Unlike a simple stimulus-response pattern, they are judgement calls guided by a large internal set of examples. You judge a situation by finding the best match between the present set of cues and those carried in the stories you remember.

The most influential cue in the environment is the behavior of others. Carnival pitchmen are notorious for using accomplices in the audience to break the ice. Everyone is afraid, looking for someone else to go first and buy the bottle of snake oil. A deacon seeds the collection plate with a ten-spot to give the congregation an example to follow. We follow the leader, sometimes in the old-brain, reptile sense, sometimes in a more reasoning manner.

I complained once to a friend about how the mechanic who inspected my car had placed the inspection sticker crookedly on my windshield. My friend replied that the piles of food wrappers and coffee stains that I left on the floor of the car probably led the mechanic to infer that I didn't care about the appearance of the car, so he did not need to expend extra effort in aesthetic considerations. It may be coincidence, but cleaning out the car prior to inspection has produced a straight sticker ever since. Cues in the environment shape behavior when they add up to a concept.

In the classic study, pedestrians at a crosswalk were more likely to cross against the light when one of the researchers did it first. They were even more likely to violate the rules when the researcher was dressed as a high-status individual. Individuals look for social proof from others before they will take action. As Max Hastings wrote of the men on Omaha beach, "Much of what happens on a battlefield is decided by example, men being driven to act in noble or ignoble fashion by the behavior of those around them."

Choosing the examples you present in your communication shapes the formation of concepts by the audience. The nineteenth-century Russian writer Turgenev changed his audience's concept of the peasant through his stories that showed their humanity and oc-

casional wisdom. If you want people to make fewer inferences that others of a certain appearance are stupid, then increase the examples that show that particular inference as an error, as well as ones that show an alternative concept as correct.

Rule Application

Teaching your audience rules gives them independent power. If you teach them the rules, they can play the game, whether it be hoops or physics. If you want to direct action over a wide range of unique but similar incidents, impart the rules of your game to your audience with clear examples of how they can be applied. Rules can also be chained. "In case of fire, use assigned stairway A, but if you see smoke or flame in that direction, use stairway B." Such guidelines increase the odds of a successful outcome under stressful circumstances. When you know the rules of etiquette (so they tell us), you are never unsure how to act in any social situation. The excellency of a rule is its versatility. If you know that, as a rule, internal combustion engines require a break-in period before they are used at full power, you are less likely to ruin any new engine that comes into your life, whether it be in a car or a lawn mower.

Local rules generate global order. If there are no rules, how can you break them? It's tennis without a net. Linear experiences have predictable outcomes; but in the free interaction, as in chess, the players respond and adapt to the moves of the other players in an ever-changing environment. You have no way to predict the moves of the players, the possible combinations of experiences, or the final outcome of the game. You offer a good game and you'll always be surprised by the outcome. The "complex adaptive system" is never settled; it is always dynamic, always evolving new connections.

Rules are not just social constructs, in that the laws of physics and such seem to operate independently of humans. Still, the rules of physics that I learned in school have changed over time, as they probably always will. If there is one rule that guides us before moving to the next step, it is the one that teaches us the limitations of knowledge and the beginnings of wisdom. Jacob Bronowski was passionate in his application of Heisenberg's uncertainty principle, or law of tolerance, to all of life. We always try to reduce uncertainty, but Heisenberg's principle shows us that we never can re-

duce it entirely. Actions against fragile life are irreversible, and it's a painfully old story how certainty and dogmatism have led rational humans into rationalized murder.

Even the rule of tolerance has to be applied in a reasonable manner; conscious-ness of it should engender progress, not paralysis. With it, and all the other uncertain rules, we can move up to the next level of audience action.

Constructive Problem Solving

You don't measure the success of a library by waiting at the exit and testing for acceptance of your personal subset of conclusions. You don't even measure the success of a single book in such a small-minded way. The creative potential of human interaction is equally too rich for such narrow results. Communi-

cation is a messy system, like the Everglades, full of meandering streams, swamps, wildlife, and complexity. Someone always wants to get in there and straighten out the mess, to channelize the meandering streams and impose linear order, but destroy the living system.

Thomas Edison once asked one of his top young assistants to find out the amount of air that would have to be pumped out of a newly designed lightbulb. Handing the young man the lightbulb, he expected the answer in a few minutes. The assistant went off with the glass bulb and did not return for hours. Finally Edison went looking for him, and found him sweating, hollow-eyed, frantically working his slide rule and calipers over drawings and measurements of the bulb. "I've almost got it. It's just that geometry of the curve in the neck that's getting me." Edison looked at the measurements, complimented the work, and then motioned for the man to follow him. Stopping at the sink, he placed the lightbulb under the tap and filled it with water through the unsealed end. He then poured the water back out into a graduated cylinder and read the results.

I like this story because it celebrates the triumph of both simplicity and complexity. Edison could have narrowed down the task. He could have told the assistant exactly how to do it and ensured success on the immediate task. He could have punished the man for taking an inefficient path to solving the problem. But Edison was building an invention factory, and the essential by-product of invention is failure. Not everything has to go through endless trial and error, but the attitude toward failure is an essential element of progress. If everything succeeds, then nothing needs to change; without failure to understand, nothing forces us to explore. Your interaction doesn't just provide information, it should nurture the habit of creating new patterns of connections. Creation emerges.

As psychologist Carl Rogers said: "We can choose to use the behavioral sciences in ways which free, not control; which will bring about constructive variability, not conformity; which will develop creativity, not contentment; which will facilitate each person in his self-directed process of becoming; which will aid individuals, groups, and even the concept of science to become self-transcending in freshly adaptive ways of meeting life and its problems."

Is allowing complex, diverse discourse and new meanings to emerge a surrender to chaos or acceptance of ultimate reality? You may have a clear destination in mind, but when you are open to new experiences along the way, you may get there by an entirely new route or somewhere else altogether. E. L. Doctorow observed that writing a novel is like driving across the country at night. Your headlights can show you only a little ways ahead, but that is enough to guide you on the whole journey. It's just a matter of trust. Trust that brings our best nature to the surface in a relationship that rises above manipulation, interaction that rises to the highest common denominator.

Sales professionals have spent countless hours perfecting their skill at "closing"—of getting that final signature on the deal. Surely you have been on the receiving end of many of these. They all have cute names: the "turnover close," the "pretend-to-leave close," all designed to trick you into action.

They are professionals, and if communication is part of what puts bread on your table, so are you. You too are concerned with getting commitments—commitments to think, to explore, to reason, and to shift perspectives. Your success comes not with closing, but with opening. No matter how authoritarian you want to be, people construct their own meaning. You can do data-dump or discovery and they will still be constructing their own meaning—the difference is how enjoyable it is. The headlights don't need to shine all the way to the destination, just a little ways ahead. When they leave you, are their gears still turning, grinding away at the mystery? When we help them consider a new idea, or inspire feeling from another perspective, when they say, "Yes, I'll try. I won't settle for certainty"— in a thousand little ways, we have earned well our hire.

CHAPTER 9
THE MORNING AFTER

The single drunken laugh from the back of the hall made the stunned silence seem even more profound. As the implications of my story of the sheep found in the inventory of the Pilgrim's bedroom sunk in, it seemed I had pulled a giant plug, draining the goodwill from the room in an instant. As I realized what I had done ("My God, I've just told a sheep joke to 383 people!"), my vision began to dissolve from color to black and white. My voice began to sound hollow and distant. My own body was disassociating from me. I stammered and stuttered my after-dinner presentation to as rapid a close as I could muster, but the horror seemed never to end. Like a car wreck in slow motion, the flying debris of my desperate words crept through the air toward my stunned audience.

Sometimes you eat the bear,
sometimes the bear eats you.

Never mind that the story about the sheep in the bedroom was true. Never mind that I had first heard it in a lecture given by one of the nation's foremost archaeologists. Never mind how well my talk had been going up to that point. The degree of trust that I had built with this audience made the betrayal even worse.

It's helpful to have the bottom of one's career so precisely defined. Rarely will you have such a clear disaster or triumph to let you know how "it went." After my sheep fiasco it was clear to me that I was best suited to be a lighthouse keeper on the north coast of Greenland. Such a hard lesson scarcely needs repeating, and I have steered clear of that brand of questionable material in the decades since. Still, there is hardly a communications disaster that I have not explored. Character is destiny, and my character is impulsive. I have studied and learned the rules of civilized discourse, but, like many, I occasionally get the notion that the rules just don't apply to me. They do.

These postpresentation feelings of doubt and regret, these realizations that come too late, are what inform you and drive you toward excellence—just don't let them drive you out of the business. No matter what you do, at least you did not tell the sheep joke.

So it's over. If it was a big presentation, you had the applause to let you know how it ended. If it was a more informal interaction, you might get a "thank-you." More important than what you get is what you give. They have given you their attention and you owe them your thanks. A thank-you is not only appropriate and expected, it lets everyone know when you're done.

But it's not over. Your audience has been changed by their time with you. They will continue to shape the experience into coherence with their personal journey, as you must now integrate it into your own path of craft mastery. To do that, you need distance and details.

This is a delicate matter. You have been the center of attention for the whole time that you were on. How will you come across if you now start begging everyone around you for feedback? Enough about you! The caravan has moved on! Wait, instead, for someone else to bring it up. If someone says, "I really enjoyed your presentation," thank them, and if there is a detail you are concerned about, ask their opinion. Say, "Thanks, I really enjoyed being here. I have to tell you, though, I was worried about the part with the 'paper or plastic' analogy. Did that come across very clearly?" The limit is one question per audience member who initiates the subject of your performance and no more.

There is no limit, however, to the questions that will come to you later. That night, go over the event in your head and find the lessons for the next time. What did you leave out? What should you have left out? Did the intensity and connection build as you had intended? Was anything offputting? Did anything come too early? On a more profound level, what did you leave your audience with? What was the general mood and message? Did you connect with their needs, or just inflict your personality on them? Did you include yourself among flawed humanity or alienate the audience with imagined superiority? These deliberate questions won't be all. The next day, usually in the tub or shower, some obvious thing that you wish you had or had not done will burst in upon your contemplation. "L'esprit de bathtub."

Write it all down. If you began with a set list, an outline of your presentation, it now has three forms: as you originally planned it, as you delivered it, and as you now think you should have delivered it. Keep your outline (as delivered and with your notes as to how it should have been) where

The opening thanks and recognizes that they are missing two popular TV shows as well as Garrison Keillor who is performing nearby.

Opening joke that occurred to me at the last minute noting that the weather is better than the previous year but cancelled out by my increasing age.

Compliment (not used) about how the rest of the world looks like a microchip from an airplane, but not this place.

Warm-up quiz game with coffee mug as prize.

An old joke about nails having heads on the wrong end. OK because I couched it as an example of an odd survivor.

Leads into "Survivor" game where guests vote one of two staff hosts out of the room. Probably too negative. (Note names written down.)

Major demo with props. Connects to accidents of survival and main topic.

Current news hooks.

Major rant and rave. Used the year before, but preceded by apology about how I had gotten out of control the year before, which leads me into doing it again.

Parody of "Trouble" from The Music Man.

10° cooler but 1 year older

—Thanks for coming

Survivor, Millionaire, Garrison - MISSING

— Looks like a micro chip - thanks

— Millionaire quiz. - bars + tone, Ken Burns

— Nail head joke

— Survivor - Galoots vs. Normites
(Kelli Falcone)   (John Guild)

— Test of time- shingles — axe

— Water on Mars - Grandad of toy

— A pologise - letter on safety glasses.

— Trouble

— Lake Wood begone — Ed Egerton

"Where all the wood is strong, all the tools good looking, and all craftsmanship above average."

Final quotation written out in full.

A "callback" to the introduction and my promise to deliver all that they are missing. Major humorous story with the final punch line modified to explain the wealth of the organization hosting the dinner.

(opposite) My outline from a 25-minute after-dinner talk given for public television and museum supporters. Some of the audience had seen me the year before, but only half of my material was new. The linking theme was survival.

you can access it over the years to come. You'll need it. First, you don't want to deliver the same stories to the same crowd when you are invited back. Second, the annotated outline is the foundation for your next gig. Outlines live in the middle range of presentations. By definition, spontaneous interactions will not have prewritten outlines, nor will oft-repeated presentations. If you repeat a presentation often enough, it can safely evolve within your long-term memory. But a talk that you might give every month or three evolves best on paper. In my case, the life cycle of the outline of an after-dinner talk is as follows.

First, I tear up the last outline I used—not into shreds, but into strips, each containing a unit of the presentation. Adding strips that take advantage of the immediate experience of the night's audience, I move them around on the hotel room desk just hours before the presentation. I put the easy, connection-building, and energizing material at the top of the list, moving on to the more challenging. When it looks like I have the right order, I either tape the notes together into a strip or transcribe them onto a single sheet with lettering bold enough to read at a glance during the presentation.

During the presentation, the outline sits in easy sight like a responsible friend, watching over me. During the actual delivery connections, linkages and insights always occur to me as I work with the audience. (It's only fair. If you allow your audience the constructive intelligence to make new connections and to find new meanings, you can certainly allow yourself the same privilege.) I also have the outline to swim back to, and that sets me free to be in the moment sharing the exhilaration of creation with the audience.

And when it's over, I (should) write it all down. This is hard to do, first of all because I'm pooped, and if things went well I'm on top of the world and don't need any stinking notes. If things did not go so well, I just want to crawl under a wet rock. But be a pro, write down your notes and help yourself along. It's an investment that pays off when you tear the revised version into strips for the next go-round.

Lying awake, thinking over "how it went," is helpful only if you're going to take action. Were you too tired? Can you exercise more or change the schedule? Was there a way to do that challenge in a more positive way? Did that family leave because of your rude pun? Did you go on automatic today, losing contact with the moment? Did you slow down and rebuild the connection? Did you let them do their work? Reflection, action, reflection, action. It's a life-long project. The ever-emerging, complex interactions with the audiences you will meet will earn your enduring astonishment. It's an endlessly fascinating craft, this business of engaging the intelligence of others. Taking your turn to lead is part of becoming fully human, as beneath your feet you feel the planet tilting in its path, shifted just a bit in its course by your courage and skill.

Notes

Chapter 1

3   *Strive to reduce our uncertainty:* Goss, 1989

3   *Play gives us a survival advantage:* Englefield, 1985

3   *Even the Federal Aviation Administration:* Woodyard, "Southwest Airlines Makes Flying Fun," USA Today, Sept. 22, 1998

4   *Greatest pleasure, that zone of growth:* Daloz, 1986; Csikszentmihalyi, 1990

7   *The ability to obtain goals:* Pinker, 1997

7   *A theory that slices intelligence:* Sternberg, 1986

10   *Engendering trust, issuing a challenge:* Daloz, 1986

Chapter 2

13   *If you were placed on trial:* Campbell, David "The Psychology of Creativity" sound recording, Greensboro, N.C. : Center for Creative Leadership, 199-?

14   *Compares creativity to the age-old advice:* Sternberg, Robert J., lecture given at Chautauqua, NY

14   *Fourth step of a five step process:* Campbell, David "The Psychology of Creativity", sound recording, Greensboro, N.C. : Center for Creative Leadership, 199-?

16   *Characteristic of the "artistic temperament":* Jamison, 1993

19   *He wondered if nature really had a master plan:* Michael Offutt, "The Chemistry Songbag", Portland, Me. : J. Weston Walch, 1991

21   *The origin of the steel "rhino" tusks:* Hastings, 1984

21   *"If an idea isn't scary":* source unknown

Chapter 3

23   *If you want to make God laugh:* Lamott, 1994

23   *Communication can be sliced:* Hollingworth, 1935

27   *Investigation, Inference & Invention:* Barton, 1989

28   *Mentors toss little bits:* Daloz, 1986

30   *Critical reflection is the intellectual habit:* Brookfield, 1995

32   *An audience of experts:* Vardaman, 1970

33   *An indifferent or resistant audience:* ibid

34 *Better suited to the hostile audience:* ibid

37 *The sequence of steps is a journey:* source unknown

38 *Struggle to say anything worthwhile:* Bolker, 1997

Chapter 4

42 *Essence of attention is contrast:* Hollingworth, 1935

43 *Salesman of the century:* Popeil, 1995

44 *You are unusual in some manner:* Kleinke, 1986

45 *Either have your learner's attention:* Jensen, 1998

47 *We can pay attention to only a very limited:* Travers, 1970; Goss, 1989

48 *The classic Maine guide of the 1940s:* Rich, Louise Dickinson. *We Took to the Woods,* New York: J. B. Lippincott, 1942

51 *Comedians once used segues to move:* Carter, 1989

52 *Echo of our evolutionary journey:* Sagan, 1977

58 *Being in groups of strangers:* Cassidy, 1999

63 *Show your genuine interest:* Goss, 1989

63 *"Your eyes belong to the audience":* source unknown

64 *"Directness and intensity":* of verbal communications: Mehabrian, 1971

66 *Sustained looking can be taken:* Kleinke, 1986

68 *People in the center and front:* Hollingworth, 1935

Chapter 5

71 *Interest is the catalyst that drives:* Ostermann, 1899

71 *Dullness is a sin:* Craddock, 1985

72 *Seven fundamental factors of interest:* from an unknown text on writing

75 *To get people to adopt the stories:* Schank, 1990, p. 217

81 *Laughing out loud:* Sylwester, 1995

82 *Began his career selling kitchen gadgets:* Popeil, 1995

82 *In the radio series "A Prairie Home Companion":* Lee, J. Y., 1991

83 *Using the joke-mapping strategy:* De Bono, 1992

84 *Henri Bergson observed that we laugh:* Sypher, 1956

84 *The deeper level of humor:* Carter, 1989

84 *Call backs, etc.:* ibid

86 *Begin to disconnect from the audience:* ibid

90 *Howard Gardner's eight intelligences:* Gardner, 1983

94 *"Colorful theater of physics":* Tufte, 1997

102 *This spectrogram and the ones that follow:* spectrograms by the author using 44.1 kHz samples

107 *Table on left brain/right brain:* after Dunn, R., et al, "Hemispheric preference: The newest element of learning style." *The American Biology Teacher,* May, 1982, pp. 292-294

Chapter 6

110 *Stories and categories:* Goss, 1989

113 *Benefit from past experience:* Schank, 1990

114 *Use clear and familiar structures:* Mambert, 1971; Vardaman, 1970

118 *Brains are conservative organs:* Goss, 1989

120 *Labeling also shapes our memory:* ibid

123 *Simple repetition of a key idea:* Hollingworth, 1935

129 *Scholars of the same period:* Carruthers, Mary, *The Book of Memory: a study of memory in medieval culture,* New York: Cambridge University Press, 1990

129 *"The advice to the teacher would be to embed":* James McGaugh interview transcript from *"Remembering What Matters"* on Scientific American Frontiers television broadcast

130 *In 1925, one former student recalled:* quoted in Shirer, William. *The Rise and Fall of the Third Reich,* New York: Simon & Schuster, 1959

Chapter 7

141 *We are more consistent in our responses:* Goss, 1989; Hollingworth, 1935

144 *Walter Lord observed this in his book:* Lord, Walter. *Day of Infamy.* New York: Henry Holt, 1957

147 *Mention that you once disagreed:* Kleinke, 1986

149 *Attorney Jerry Spence always tries:* Spence, 1995

149 *Highly empathic people can succeed:* Brooks, 1989

151 *In 1939, when exiled European scientists:* Rhodes, Richard. *The Making of the Atomic Bomb.* New York: Simon & Schuster, 1998

151 *Galileo made enemies:* Reston, 1994

155 *Innately fine-tuned to detect cheaters:* Pinker, 1997

156 *Convincing liars:* Kleinke, 1986

158 *Perceived scarcity of the expertise:* Nations, Howard L. *Powerful Persuasion*, text published on internet

163 *Galileo had the evidence of the telescope:* Reston, 1994

175 *A woman needs a man:* quoted in Sagan, 1996

Chapter 8

180 *People as curious primates:* Gould, 1996

181 *Yerkes-Dodson law:* Goldstein & Krasner, 1987

182 *Habituation is combat training:* Cassidy, 1999

184 *If they are having too much trouble:* Goldstein & Krasner, 1987, p. 206

185 *We revert to lower brain function:* Jensen, 1998

188 *Hierarchy proposed by psychologist Robert M. Gagné:* Gagné, 1965

188 *Tab A slot B:* Hollingworth, 1935

192 *Tasks have dimensions:* Norman, 1988

192 *Activities that are wide and deep:* Norman, 1988; Reeves, 1999

195 *Watch intrinsically motivated hobbyists:* Koelsnick, 1975; Detterman & Sternberg, 1993

196 *Pedestrians at a crosswalk:* Karlins, et. al., 1972

196 *"Much of what happens on a battlefield":* Hastings, 1984

198 *Jacob Bronowski was passionate:* Bronowski, Jacob. *The Ascent of Man.* Boston: Little, Brown and Company, 1973

200 *"We can choose to use the behavioral sciences":* excerpt in Karlins & Andrews, 1972, p. 258

BIBLIOGRAPHY

Adger, Carolyn Temple, et al. *Engaging Students: Thinking, Talking, Creating*. Thousand Oaks, CA: Corwin Press, Inc., 1995

Barton, R. *Acting: Onstage and Off*. Orlando, FL: Holt, Rinehart and Winston, Inc., 1989

Berger, Arthur Asa. *Narratives in Popular Culture, Media, and Everyday Life*. Thousand Oaks, CA: Sage Publications, 1997

Bolker, Joan, ed. *The Writer's Home Companion*. New York: Henry Holt, 1997

Book, Casandra L., et al. *Human Communication: Principles, Contexts, and Skills*. New York: St. Martin's Press Inc., 1980

Brookfield, Stephen D. *The Skillful Teacher: On Technique, Trust, and Responsiveness in the Classroom*. San Francisco: Jossey-Bass Inc., 1990

————. *Becoming a Critically Reflective Teacher*. San Francisco: Jossey-Bass Inc., 1995

Brooks, Michael. *Instant Rapport*. New York: Warner Books, Inc., 1989

Caine, Renate Numella and Caine, Geoffrey. *Making Connections: Teaching and the Human Brain*. Alexandria, VA: Association for Supervision and Curriculum Development, 1991

Capaldi, Nicholas. *The Art of Deception: An Introduction to Critical Thinking*. Amherst, NY: Prometheus Books, 1987

Carter, Judy. *Stand-Up Comedy: The Book*. New York: Dell Publishing, 1989

Cassidy, Tony. *Stress, Cognition and Health*. London: Routledge, 1999

Chiario, Delia. *The Language of Jokes: Analysing Verbal Play*. London: Routledge, 1992

Cialdini, Robert B. *Influence: The Psychology of Persuasion*. New York: William Morrow & Company, 1993

Cole, Toby, ed. *Acting, A Handbook of the Stanislavski Method*. New York: Crown Publishers, Inc., 1955

Costa, Arthur L. & Liebmann, R. M., eds. *Envisioning Process as Content: Towards a Renaissance Curriculum*. Thousand Oaks, CA: Corwin Press, Inc., 1997

Covey, S. *The Seven Habits of Highly Effective People*. New York: Simon & Schuster, 1989

Craddock, Fred B. *Preaching*. Nashville, TN: Abingdon Press, 1985

Csikszentmihalyi, M. *Flow, The Psychology of Optimal Experience*. New York: Harper & Row, 1990

Daloz, Laurent A. *Effective Teaching and Mentoring*. San Francisco: Jossey-Bass, 1986

De Bono, Edward. *Serious Creativity, Using the Power of Lateral Thinking to Create New Ideas*. New York: HarperBusiness, 1992

DeCarvalho, Roy José. *The Growth Hypothesis in Psychology: The Humanistic Psychology of Abraham Maslow and Carl Rogers*. San Francisco: Mellen Research University Press, 1991

DePorter, Bobbi. *Quantum Learning: Unleashing the Genius in You*. New York: Dell Publishing, 1992

Detterman, Douglas K. & Sternberg, Robert J., eds. *Transfer on Trial: Intelligence, Cognition and Instruction*. Norwood, NJ: Ablex Publishing Co., 1993

Eagleton, Terry. *Literary Theory, An Introduction*. Minneapolis, MN: University of Minnesota Press, 1983

Edwards, Betty. *Drawing on the Right Side of the Brain*. Los Angeles: J. P. Tarcher, Inc., 1979

Englefield, Ronald. *The Mind at Work and Play*. Buffalo, NY: Prometheus Books, 1985

Falk, John H. & Dierking, Lynn D. *The Museum Experience*. Washington, DC: Whalesback Books, 1992

Field, Syd. *Screenplay, The Foundations of Screenwriting*. New York: Dell Publishing, 1982

Fine, Elizabeth C. and Speer, Jean H., eds. *Performance, Culture, and Identity*. Westport, CT: Praeger Publishers, 1992

Fischer, David Hackett. *Historians' Fallacies: Towards a Logic of Historical Thought*. New York: Harper & Row, Publishers, 1970

Flesch, Rudolf. *How to Write, Speak and Think More Effectively*. New York: Signet, 1960

Fletcher, Leon. *How to Speak Like a Pro*. New York: Ballantine Books, 1983

Frank, Milo O. *How to Get Your Point Across in 30 Seconds or Less*. New York: Simon & Schuster, 1986

Funkhouser, G. Ray. *The Power of Persuasion: A Guide to Moving Ahead in Business & Life*. New York: Times Books, 1986

Gagné, Robert M. *The Conditions of Learning and Theory of Instruction*. New York: Holt, Rinehart & Winston, 1965

Gardner, Howard. *Frames of Mind, The Theory of Multiple Intelligences*. New York: Basic Books, 1983

————. *Leading Minds: An Anatomy of Leadership*. New York: Basic Books, 1995

Gaulke, Sue. *One Hundred and One Ways to Captivate a Business Audience*. New York: AMACOM, 1997

Gelb, Michael J. *Present Yourself*. Torrance, CA: Jalmar Press, 1988

Goldberg, Natalie. *Writing Down the Bones*. Boston: Shambhala Publications, Inc., 1986

Goldstein, Arnold P. & Krasner, Leonard. *Modern Applied Psychology*. Elmsford, NY: Pergamon Books, 1987

Goss, Blaine. *The Psychology of Human Communication*. Prospect Heights, IL: Waveland Press, Inc., 1989

Gould, Stephen Jay. *Full House, The Spread of Excellence from Plato to Darwin*. New York: Harmony Books, 1996

Grinder, Alison L. and McCoy, Sue E. *The Good Guide: A Sourcebook for Interpreters, Docents and Tour Guides*. Scottsdale, AZ: Ironwood Publishing, 1985

Gross, Robert. *Peak Learning*. Los Angeles: Jeremy P. Tarcher, Inc., 1991

Gullette, Margaret M., ed. *The Art and Craft of Teaching*. Cambridge, MA: Harvard University Press, 1984

Hastings, Max. Overloard: *D-Day and the Battle for Normandy*. New York: Simon & Schuster, 1984

Hoff, Ron. *"I Can See You Naked" A Fearless Guide to Making Great Presentations*. New York: Andrews and McMeel, 1988

————. *Say It In Six, How to Say Exactly What You Mean in Six Minutes or Less*. Kansas City, MO: Andrews and McMeel, 1996

Hollingworth, H. L. *The Psychology of the Audience*. New York: American Book Company, 1935

Hunsaker, Phillip L. and Alessandra, Anthony J. *The Art of Managing People*. New York: Simon & Schuster, Touchstone, 1986

Jamison, Kay Redfield. *Touched With Fire: Manic Depressive Illness and the Artistic Temperament*. New York: The Free Press, 1993

Jensen, Eric. *Sizzle & Substance, Presenting with the Brain in Mind*. San Diego: The Brain Store, 1998

————. *Teaching with the Brain in Mind*. Alexandria, VA: Association for Supervision and Curriculum Development, 1998

Johnston, Deirdre D. *The Art and Science of Persuasion*. Dubuque: Brown & Benchmark, 1994

Jolles, Robert L. *How to Run Seminars and Workshops: Presentation Skills for Consultants, Trainers, and Teachers*. New York: John Wiley & Sons, 1994

Karlins, M. and Andrews, L., eds. *Man Controlled: Readings in the Psychology of Behavior Control*. New York: The Free Press, 1972

Kawasaki, Guy. *Selling the Dream*. New York: HarperCollins, 1992

Kleinke, C. *Meeting & Understanding People: How to Develop Competence in Social Situations and Expand Social Skills*. New York: W. H. Freeman & Company, 1986

Klopf, A. Harry. *The Hedonistic Neuron: A Theory of Memory, Learning, and Intelligence*. Washington: Hemisphere Publishing, 1982

Kolesnik, Walter B. *Humanism and/or Behaviorism in Education*. Boston: Allyn & Bacon, Inc., 1975

Lamott, Anne. *Bird by Bird: Some Instructions on Writing and Life*. New York: Doubleday, 1994

Langer, Ellen J. *Mindfulness*. Reading, MA: Addison-Wesley Publishing Co., 1989

—————. *The Power of Mindful Learning*. Reading, MA: Addison-Wesley Publishing Co., 1997

Lee, Alfred M. and Lee, Elizabeth B. *The Fine Art of Propaganda: A Study of Father Coughlin's Speeches*. New York: Harcourt, Brace and Company, 1939

Lee, Judith Yaross. *Garrison Keillor, A Voice of America*. Jackson, MS: University Press of Mississippi, 1991

Lewis, William J. *Interpreting for Park Visitors*. Yorktown, VA: Eastern National Park & Monument Association, 1980

Loughary, John W. and Hopson, Barrie. *Producing Workshops, Seminars, and Short Courses: A Trainer's Handbook*. Chicago: Follett Publishing Company, 1979

Maidment, Robert. *Straight Talk: A Guide to Saying More With Less*. Gretna, LA: Pelican Publishing Co., 1982

Mambert, W. A. *Elements of Effective Communication*. Washington, DC: Acropolis Books, 1971

Mandler, Jean M. *Stories, Scripts, and Scenes: Aspects of Schema Theory*. Hillsdale, NJ: Lawrence Earlbaum Associates, Publishers, 1984

Marsh, P. *Eye to Eye, How People Interact.* Topsfield, MA: Salem House, 1988

Martin, Garry and Martin, Pear. *Behavior Modification.* Englewood Cliffs, NJ: Prentice-Hall, 1983

Maslow, Abraham H. *Maslow on Management.* New York: John Wiley & Sons, Inc., 1998

McDonald, Daniel. *Language of Argument.* New York: HarperCollins College Publishers, 1993

Mehabrian, Albert. *Silent Messages.* Belmont, CA: Wadsworth Publishing, 1971

Milhollan, Frank and Forisha, Bill E. *From Skinner to Rogers: Contrasting Approaches to Education.* Lincoln, NE: Professional Educators Publications, Inc., 1972

Mira, Thomas K. *Speak Smart.* New York: Princeton Review Publishing, 1997

Morowitz, H. J. and Singer, J. L. eds., *The Mind, The Brain, and Complex Adaptive Systems.* Reading MA: Addison Wesley, 1995

Morrisey, G.L., Sechrest, T. L. and Warman, W. B. *Loud and Clear.* Reading, MA: Addison Wesley, 1997

Nirenberg, Jesse S. *Getting Through to People.* Englewood Cliffs, NJ: Prentice-Hall, Inc., 1963

Norman, Donald A. *The Psychology of Everyday Things.* New York: Basic Books, 1988

Ostermann, Wilhelm. *Interest in its Relation to Pedagogy.* New York: E. L. Kellogg & Co., 1899

Peoples, David. *Presentations Plus.* New York: John Wiley & Sons, 1992

Petty, Richard E., Ostrom, Thomas M., and Brock, Timothy C. eds., *Cognitive Responses in Persuasion.* Hillsdale, NJ: Lawrence Erlbaum Associates, Publishers, 1981

Pfarrer, Don. *Guerrilla Persuasion.* New York: Houghton Mifflin, 1998

Pinker, Steven. *How the Mind Works.* New York: W. W. Norton Co., 1997

Pont, Tony. *Developing Effective Training Skills.* London: McGraw-Hill Book Company, 1991

Popeil, Ron and Graham, Jefferson. *The Salesman of the Century.* New York: Dell Publishing, 1995

Postman, Neil. *Amusing Ourselves to Death: Public Discourse in the Age of Show Business.* New York: Viking Penguin, Inc., 1985

Poulter, C. *Playing the Game.* Studio City, CA: Players Press, 1991

Read, Hadley. *Communication: Methods for All Media.* Urbana, IL: University of Illinois Press, 1972

Reay, David G. *Understanding How People Learn.* East Brunswick, NJ: Nichols Publishing, 1994

Reeves, Wayne. *Learner-Centered Design.* Thousand Oaks, CA: Sage Publications, 1999

Reston Jr., James. *Galileo: A Life.* New York, HarperCollins, 1994

Roberts, Lisa C. *From Knowledge to Narrative: Educators and the Changing Museum.* Washington: Smithsonian Institution Press, 1997

Rogers, Carl R. *Freedom to Learn.* Columbus, OH: Charles E. Merrill Publishing Company, 1969

Roth, Stacy F. *Past into Present: Effective Techniques for First-Person Historical Interpretation.* Chapel Hill : The University of North Carolina Press, 1998

Rutter, D. R. *Looking and Seeing: The Role of Visual Communication in Social Interaction.* New York: John Wiley & Sons, 1984

Sagan, Carl. *The Dragons of Eden: Speculations on the Evolution of Human Intelligence.* New York: Ballantine Books, 1977

————. *Broca's Brain, Reflections on the Romance of Science.* New York: Ballantine Books, 1979

————. *The Demon-Haunted World: Science as a Candle in the Dark.* New York: Ballantine Books, 1996

Sandell, Rolf. *Linguistic Style and Persuasion.* London: Academic Press, 1997

Sarafina, Edward P. *Principles of Behavior Change.* New York: John Wiley & Sons Inc., 1996

Schank, Roger C. *Tell Me A Story.* New York: Charles Scribner's Sons, 1990

Shamas, Laura Annawyn. *Playwriting for Theater, Film,* White Hall, VA: Betterway Publications, 1991

Slutsky, Jeff and Aun, Michael. *The Toastmasters International Guide to Successful Speaking.* Chicago: Dearborn Financial Publishing, 1997

Snow Stephen Eddy. *Performing the Pilgrims.* Jackson: University Press of Mississippi, 1993

Spence, Gerry. *How to Argue and Win Every Time.* New York: St. Martin's Press, 1995

Spolin, Viola. *Improvisation for the Theater.* Evanston, IL: Northwestern University Press, 1963

Stearns, Peter N. *Meaning Over Memory: Recasting the Teaching of Culture and History.* Chapel Hill : The University of North Carolina Press, 1993

Steffe, Leslie P. and Gale, Jerry, eds. *Constructivism in Education.* Hillsdale, NJ: Lawrence Erlbaum Associates, Publishers, 1995

Sternberg, Robert J. *Intelligence Applied: Understanding and Increasing Your Intellectual Skills.* San Diego: Harcourt Brace Jovanovich, 1986

——————. *Wisdom: Its Nature, Origins, and Development.* New York: Cambridge University Press, 1990

Sternberg, Robert J. and Spear-Swerling, Louise. *Teaching for Thinking.* Washington, DC: American Psychological Association, 1996

Sylwester, Robert. *A celebration of neurons : an educator's guide to the human brain.* Alexandria, Va. : Association for Supervision and Curriculum Development, 1995

Sypher, Wylie ed., *Comedy.* Baltimore: The Johns Hopkins University Press, 1956

Tauber, Robert T. and Mester, Cathy S. *Acting Lessons for Teachers: Using Performance Skills in the Classroom.* Westport, CT: Prager Publishers, 1994

Tizard, Leslie J. *Preaching, The Art of Communication.* New York: Oxford University Press, 1959

Travers, Robert M. W. *Man's Information System.* Scranton, PA: Chandler Publishing Company, 1970

Tufte, Edward Rolf. *Visual Explanations.* Cheshire, CT: Graphics Press, 1997

Vardaman, George T. *Effective Communication of Ideas.* New York: Van Nostrand Reinhold, 1970

Walters, Dottie and Walters, Lilly. *Speak and Grow Rich.* New York: Prentice-Hall, 1997

Walters, Lilly. *Secrets of Successful Speakers.* New York: McGraw-Hill, 1993

Walton, Douglas. *The Place of Emotion in Argument.* University Park, PA: The Pennsylvania State University Press, 1992

Weber, E. *Vision, Composition and Photography.* New York: Walter de Gruyter, 1978

Willett, John. *The Theatre of Bertolt Brecht.* London: Eyre Methuen Ltd., 1977

Witz, Marion. *Stand Up and Talk to 1000 People (And Enjoy It!).* Toronto: McLeod Publishing, 1997

Zissner, William. *On Writing Well.* New York: HarperPerennial, 1976

INDEX

About the Author

Born in Washington, D.C., Roy Underhill holds a B.F.A. in directing from the University of North Carolina at Chapel Hill (1972) and a M.F. from Duke University (1975). He is best known as the creator and host of the PBS series *The Woodwright's Shop*, one of the longest running programs in the history of television. He is the author of five books and scores of articles on early technology. As Director of Interpretive Development for the Colonial Williamsburg Foundation, he developed award-winning programs and developed new training programs in presentation skills. He continues his work in the craft of communication through extensive consulting, training, and speaking engagements. He lives in Williamsburg, VA.

SCHOOL OF EDUCATION
CURRICULUM LABORATORY
UM-DEARBORN

Printed in the United States
152505LV00003B/131/A

9 780738 206721